GOAL MIND™

YOUR ULTIMATE GUIDE TO SETTING AND ACHIEVING EVERY GOAL YOU CAN IMAGINE

GARY WESTFAL

BEST-SELLING AUTHOR

Foreword by Bill Crow
Chief Master Sergeant, USAF Retired

Also, by Gary Westfal

333

FEAR IS A THIEF

KEY HORIZON

DREAM OPERATIVE

G-Life Enterprises Corp.

Goal Mind

Copyright © 2020 by Gary Westfal

To receive a free e-mail newsletter delivering relevant and personally-empowering content about how to get more out of life, register directly at **GaryWestfal.com**.

ISBN: 978-0-9992220-3-4 (Paperback)
ISBN: 978-1-7351773-0-4 (Hardcover)
ISBN: 978-0-9992220-7-2 (Ebook)

Library of Congress Number: 2018912135

BOOK DESIGN BY: G-Life Enterprises Corporation
Gary Westfal, Concept Art
Anssi Lähteenoja, Concept Art
Justin Park, Graphic Artist
Scott Grinnell, Graphic Artist
Janeen Westfal, Photographer

All image permissions have been secured and/or released for use by their originator or rightful owner and documentation is on file with the publisher.

The quotes contained in this book are the original inspired thoughts of the author unless otherwise appropriately cited.

Printed in the United States of America

This book is dedicated to my grandchildren
Makayla, Micah, Alex, Jett, and Scarlett

May all your hopes, dreams, and aspirations be realized through the
achievement of each and every goal you set.

Praise for Goal Mind

"Gary Westfal has succeeded in making the power of Goal-Setting and Achievement understandable and easily applicable. *Goal Mind* is a step-by-step process that takes you from vision and purpose to application and measurement. Gary has successfully drawn from the likes of Jim Rohn, Tony Robbins, and others to allow you to succeed and soar immediately. It is a must use for all my companies."

~ Dr. Tom Roselle, Chairman of International College of Applied Kinesiology, radio talk show host, wellness facility director, and international educator

"Very early in the book, Gary hits on something I've always believed so strongly in. The best way to achieve your goals is by helping others achieve theirs. He then goes on to provide an amazing blueprint for goal-setting. He spends little time on the why, but gets right to the how, which is where we struggle. One of the most tactical books on goal-setting I've seen!"

~ Quint Studer, Founder of the Studer Group, Owner of the Pensacola Blue Wahoos Baseball Team

"Life success, no matter how you measure it, always begins with the end in mind. However, vision is not enough, passion is not enough, desire is not enough…you must analyze, plan, focus, implement, and persevere. Westfal's *Goal Mind* provides direction and serves as a roadmap for the journey of life success. All the tools are included and simply explained for the proper navigation of your goals. A must-read for those just starting out or well into their own journey.

~ Dr. Shawn Leatherman, DC, CCST, CCSP, FCBP, CMVI

"People have a passion for significance, Gary Westfal's *Goal Mind* provides a very thoughtful approach to harnessing one's passion and putting it into action. Most people have heard the adage… you can't get there if you don't know where you're going. This book is the best I've ever read on how to define where you want to go and how to get there."

~ **Lieutenant General Bradley Heithold USAF (retired)**

"Those who achieve greatness are not lucky. They develop a mindset and follow a proven plan that has existed for centuries. In *Goal Mind*, Gary Westfal shows you how to develop that mindset and execute a clear and compelling plan to achieve the life you so richly deserve."

~ **Mike Huckabee, Former Governor of Arkansas, Former United States Presidential Candidate, Radio and Television Talk Show Host, Minister**

"A clear, step-by-step plan for a life of enjoyment and success through goal-setting and accomplishment. You motivate and inspire me to do a better job in my life and my relationships."

~ **Sandy Sansing, Businessman, Philanthropist**

Acknowledgements

There are a multitude of moving pieces that must be considered during the publishing process that far exceeds the ability of one person, other than the author, to handle each and every aspect. For that reason, it is imperative to call upon the assistance and collaboration of others to ensure there is balance, relevance, and clarity in the message.

To those who unselfishly dedicated the time to create and refine the cover concept, graphics, and layout; specifically, the infinity concept, logo, and design, the inspiration of which came from the brilliant mind of my Finnish friend, **Anssi Lähteenoja**, who described the concept and content of *Goal Mind* as *a representation of the infinite power of the human mind.* And to the graphic artist who created and added the extraordinary golden touch to the infinity symbol, **Justin Park**. Gentlemen, I am extraordinarily grateful to you both.

To my closest and most trusted source of strength, comfort, support, and love—my soulmate, who doubles as my teammate—**Janeen Westfal**. You have supported my writing passion for more than a decade now. You edit, analyze, strategize, and (lovingly) criticize the entirety of the efforts behind the processes that keep our hopes, dreams, goals, and aspirations alive through the messages we carry to the masses. I am eternally grateful for your insight, your perspective, your guidance, your joy, and your love.

To the professionals and celebrities who trusted me and believe in the content and context of this book enough to have offered the credibility of their endorsement, I am honored and humbled. Your willingness to support the message will bring greater visibility to those whose lives will be affected, changed, or outright transformed by your subtle but significant nod of approval of the principles, philosophies, and practices of goal achievement. **Dr. R. Thomas Roselle**, owner and founder of the Roselle Center for Healing, and former personal physician to Anthony Robbins—your most precious commodity is time. Despite the demand for your time as a healer, you elected to be the first to place this book on your reading list and took the additional time to provide the treasured feedback and encouragement of the true professional I have come to know and respect since the dawn of our friendship. Thank you!

To everyone who took the time to provide input and encouraging feedback on the book cover layout market testing via social media, e-mail, and direct contact, thank you! Your overwhelming and enthusiastic support helped shape what eventually evolved as the awesome cover layout you now see. I couldn't be happier with the results.

Foreword

By
William Crow
Chief Master Sergeant, USAF (ret)
Pastor, First Southern Baptist Church of Warren
Bisbee, Arizona

In the course of my years, I have had the good fortune (or dumb luck) to spend thirty years of that time in military service to our country, mostly as an air traffic controller in the United States Air Force. I spent my first six years on active duty as a security police officer, but soon discovered that this initial career choice and I were not well suited for each other. During that time, I experienced what us cops collectively referred to as "the daily grind"—an unfulfilling existence without passion, purpose, or any real sense of job satisfaction. Even as a young man in a new career field I could tell something was missing. I had a desire for more but wasn't exactly certain how or where to find it. What I *did* know was that *something* had to change.

I was married with four daughters and had no clear goals for the future. I loved the Air Force, but I did *not* love my job. Fortunately, I discovered an opportunity to change things when a selection of new career fields became available for me to cross-train—one of which was *air traffic control*. It was the only new career choice that actually sounded both intriguing and a bit intimidating, which was enough for me to be attracted to it in a strange sort of way. I did my research, spoke with a few air traffic controllers, and weighed my options. Before committing, I reached out to a fellow security policeman who had been through the process of retraining into air traffic control and failed. His advice to me was to stay where it was safe and familiar. "The washout rate is high," he said. "You'd be better off to remain a cop."

I also remember a conversation I had with a law enforcement supervisor who was miserable in his job. In retrospect, my selection of "wise counselors" did little, if anything, to help me find the clarity I was desperately in search of. Things became more apparent, however, when I asked this supervisor why he didn't just choose to do something different, since he was so miserable. He told me how he was *only* six years away from retirement and a lifelong pension he was determined to achieve. Despite his dissatisfaction, he was comfortable, and he was not about to disrupt his life with such a "radical" decision. I remember how confused I was with his answer, as I found it difficult to understand how someone could knowingly spend that much more time immersed in something they despised so much.

In contrast, when I interviewed air traffic controllers, I discovered a group of people who were passionate about their job. Not only were they being paid better through bonuses and incentives, but they actually enjoyed what they were doing. Their enthusiasm was contagious and was enough to convince me to take action, establish a new goal, and work hard to learn all I could to change my future. In the process, I discovered something new about myself—a burning desire to excel and become a greater version of myself.

For the first time, I discovered an ability to look beyond my immediate circumstances as I discovered a passion that I never truly realized I had. The end game, for me, was a rewarding and successful new career path that took me places I could only dream of beforehand. I didn't realize it at the time, but in hindsight I now understand that much of what I was going through was a personal growth period to my own season of changes. A fresh new mindset would lead me to many new opportunities, rewarding experiences, and influential people as I continued to transform myself at every twist and turn of life. Among the many influential people I have been blessed to encounter along the way was a young air traffic controller by the name of Gary Westfal.

I first met Gary several years ago while serving in the Air Force together at a Florida assignment. I was immediately struck by the knowledge and passion he had for his work as an air traffic controller and the dedication he had for ensuring the mission was both safe and expeditious. His "service-first" mindset was refreshing, especially when contrasted against the "daily grind" mindset I had become used to during the first six years of my Air Force career. But, even beyond that, Gary seemed to attract what I would call *peer respect* among the other air traffic controllers because of who he was as a person. Over time, it was easy to see why. He was (and remains) the epitome of self-discipline, honesty, and integrity—a truly exceptional human being who demonstrates a genuine love of people and an intense desire for the well-being of others. And now, his incredible insight and life experience of personal development and goal achievement has found its way into an exceptional book—*Goal Mind!*

Prepare to embark on an unforgettable journey to the greatest discovery you will ever make—a discovery of your *best* self. Throughout the pages of this book, you will find ways to realign yourself with your God-given gifts and talents, leading to a direct connection with your life's purpose. As a result, you will develop a goal-getter's mindset that will lead you to so much more of what you desire in life as you begin to enjoy the fruits of your labor with far greater joy and personal satisfaction than you could ever imagine.

Success is an ambiguous concept—as it should be—because of its personally-defined nature. But the term has also found its way into a misguided narrative that must be duly recognized and addressed. The *world* often tells us that success is measured in the accumulation of dollars over the course of a career or lifetime. Pop culture attempts to convince us that success is defined by the numbers of "likes" on the pages of social media platforms or the number of fans following an artist or sports figure. There's certainly nothing wrong with making money or becoming famous, and perhaps that's your goal. But success can be defined in so many more amazing and wonderful ways. The practical and methodical approach captured in this book will help you to see beyond the confined conventional paradigms of success. In fact, that's the beauty of it all. *You* get to decide what that looks like. This book will remind you of that and show you many other ways to help you see things even clearer.

The philosophies, quotes, questions, and stories in each chapter will challenge you to consider the possibilities of a future limited *only* by your own imagination and one that encompasses the physical, spiritual, and material goals that you may have only dreamed of achieving in the past. You will also learn how to transform your dreams and desires from wishes and hopes to actionable goals you can rely on to bring about a life defined by your terms.

Goal Mind is a go-to collection of practical, thought-provoking, and actionable ideas, concepts, and philosophies that will resonate with you as a foundational truth. As a Life Coach and Pastor, I have found the wisdom contained in this book to be an invaluable source of information I provide to my clients and congregants. I look forward to watching them rise to the pinnacle of their own personal goals as I share the superb insight and ideas that will invariably lead them to their own goal mindedness and the fulfillment of their life aspirations. And that, to me, has made all the difference.

The exciting possibilities to *your own* version of success awaits. When it's all said and done, I'm confident you'll be as happy as I was to have read this book. After all, a revolutionary transformation of your life begins…*right now!*

Table of Contents

Preface

The infinite nature of our mind allows us to see with great clarity that which we desire to see. We are infinitely free to imagine, analyze, plan, and act based on what we perceive—through our minds—to be the best benefit to our own growth and self-preservation. It is for this fundamental reason I chose the infinity symbol to serve as an anchor for the cover of this book. It came to me as I called out for an idea or inspiration that best served my intent to convey the one message I hope and trust you will embrace, whether you stop reading right here or immerse yourself into the rich content that awaits. And that message is simply this:

The infinite nature of your mind
holds everything you hope to know,
achieve, learn, love, and become.

The premise of this book is based on a philosophy I have tried to live by since I first began to benefit from the principles it contains. The great inspirational orator, Zig Ziglar, famously said, *"If we are willing to help enough other people get what they want out of life, we will always get what we want."* A deeper look at this quote tells us that the essence of these words speaks to a mindset of humble, honorable, and sincere service toward others. As we begin to see the virtues and value of service, we begin to see with greater clarity how profound a philosophy this truly is. So, it is with a sincere and passionate intent that I now pass along to you the wisdom that has changed my life in so many wonderful and amazing ways. And it can change yours, too!

If you are ready to tap into your greatest potential and start realizing your greatest achievements, then this book is for you. If you are looking for ways to accelerate the pace of your success while reducing the likelihood of mistakes, frustration, and setbacks, then you will be happy you have been led to this very moment in which we find ourselves. The principles and philosophies contained in the pages of this book will save you years of arduous work and frustration in your pursuit of achievement because of those of us who have traveled the path ahead of you. Each one of us has left clues that, when acted upon, will ignite your imagination, encourage you to keep going, and convince you that you, too, can achieve any goal you set your mind to.

I have practiced every one of the principles contained in this book and have seen the results first-hand. I was not born with an ability or natural affinity for achievement or success. I was not born into wealth nor was I provided any kind of inside secrets that only the rich and famous know, aside from what you read here in these pages. My quest began with a simple curiosity and a burning desire to discover the difference between achievers and non-achievers. Like you, I had to look for answers by taking action and paying close attention to opportunity, insight, wisdom, and the subtle clues as they appeared. Make no mistake, whatever you seek *will* come to pass. Your primary responsibility at that point will be *recognition* and *action*. The philosophies and recommendations in this book will help you formulate a plan, recognize opportunity, and compel you to act, bringing you the results that have eluded you for far too long.

An Opportunity

Contrary to popular belief, opportunities are all around us *all* the time. If that were not the case then there would be no innovation, no creation, no love, no...happiness. Opportunities are an essential part of life that manifest in many ways and forms. What opportunities do *you* desire? What opportunities will *you* seize?

You are not here by mistake. The fact that you are holding this book or listening to the audio version is not happenstance. It is an opportunity. Somewhere along the line of your life's journey, you called for answers. You recognized something when you saw the title of this book. I would even go so far as to say the infinity symbol on the cover of this book *could* have played a role by connecting with the curious nature of your mind to bring you closer to the truth you seek. After all, curiosity is a rather amazingly alluring concept. Whether the title or the symbol (or both), *something* spoke to your desire for *more* that has driven you to the precipice of discovery. Whatever your dreams, goals, or aspirations, life has prompted a fundamental personal desire for achievement, the likes of which require your ability to fully understand the concept of goals. And here you are.

Time, as we understand it, is a highly perishable and precious aspect of our lives. What a tragedy it would be to have *no* resources whatsoever to accelerate your learning and comprehension curve on how best to reach your goals and save some of that precious time. Careful and practical examination of the philosophies, concepts, and strategies in this book will provide clarity, insight, and inspiration on what others have discovered to be a pathway to their success. Instead of consuming your valuable time searching for answers, this book will give you the tools to lay out a plan *right now* to begin building your dreams through the effective application of goal-setting and goal-getting. And you will do it faster, better, and far more efficiently than those who are still searching for answers.

It has been long said that an average person with clear goals will outrun any challenger who is uncertain of the direction of their goals or life purpose. IQ is insignificant, as is privilege or social status. What is and remains significant is a clearly-defined destination (a goal) and a well-defined plan to get there. This book will help you put it all into perspective!

Introduction

The successful achievement of your goals is not only possible but *certain*. I realize that's a pretty bold statement to place at the beginning of a book, but as we put things into perspective and begin to understand the concepts and foundational principles of setting and achieving goals, you will quickly realize the statement is not as bold as it first appears. Rather, it is a logical conclusion to the effective employment of the concepts and philosophies of success and achievement. The only caveat to the sentiment of certainty rests with your resolve to bring about your goals through the effective application of the principles that bring them to fruition. In other words, you must *act* on them.

Goals that have personal meaning reflect an individual's identity. Your goals address a dynamic range of self-defined ideals and basic needs that are most closely aligned with what psychoanalysts refer to as our "true self." Because your goals reflect your personal identity, you are more likely to put forth a sustained effort and focus over time. It's important to draw a distinction at this point between personal, true-self goals and those that are derived from external factors such as social influences. Externally-driven goals tend to be short-lived and are more likely to be abandoned as obstacles appear. So, take note the next time you contemplate your goals. Determine whether they are personally aligned to your true self or ones you are unlikely to follow through with and finish. You can avoid a lot of frustration and save a lot of time by conducting an honest analysis as you create new goals and consider whether or not they are worthy of your time and effort. Do only that which brings you joy and fulfillment and you will *never* be disappointed.

It is far better (and much easier) to be drawn to a goal than to have to push yourself to achieve it.

While this book focuses primarily on individual or personal goals, many of the concepts and philosophies can be applied to a collaborative, team construct as well. A common understanding of the concepts by individual members adds to the overall awareness of the team and can serve as an effective force multiplier for the advancement of ideas, innovation, and relevant and enduring change.

The Power of Goals

The power of setting goals came relatively early for me. In hindsight, the very first lesson was one that I now look back upon and smile as I consider the awesome nature of how goals truly work. I was in the ninth grade, attending a high school I had no interest in being a part of. I was there not by choice but by circumstance. Our family had recently moved to a small town outside of Jacksonville, Florida because of a job assignment one of my parents had accepted. I was an outsider and was determined to find a way to remove that distinction, so I made a bold move and joined the freshman football team. As it turns out, it was a decision that changed the course of my life. I was not an instant success. I was skinny, had no idea how to actually *play* football—aside from what I saw on television—and could hardly bench press my own bodyweight.

I remember my first discussion with the freshman football coach who—after assessing my lack of skill, knowledge, and strength—candidly announced that I would either quit before the season *began* or I'd become a new person. I liked the sound of the second option but had no clue what it would take to get there. I accepted his challenge and was told to be on the field after school for the first practice.

Cool, practice! I thought it would be something close to a pickup game I'd experienced on occasion in the neighborhood. Not even close! By the time we were finished for the day I was worn out, beat up, and dejected. The thoughts that ran through my mind that day ranged from quitting the team and running away from home, to finding a valid reason to preserve my dignity by discovering some kind of physical affliction that would legitimately disqualify me as a player. Just before I summoned the courage to talk with the coach about my options, one of the more seasoned players walked past, slapped me on the shoulder, and said, "Great practice today." I think it was when he saw the tired, dejected, and confused look on my face that he paused to tell me how the first two weeks were always the toughest. "It's when most people quit," he confided. "The coaches are looking for weakness," he added. "See you tomorrow?" I smiled through the pain, the dirt, and the sweat, and nodded affirmatively.

I wasn't very successful that first year, but I learned a lot of valuable lessons that carried me through an extremely difficult first season, both on and off the field. The lessons set me up for success the following three years of my high school football and academic years and well into the course of my adult life. I still look back upon that time as one of the most pivotal in my life because it is when I first began to discover how to set goals. I also learned how to work well with others, to look past obstacles, and to function as part of a team—all elements of an effective goal attainment strategy.

A Transformation

Determined not to be defeated, I worked hard on my mind—learning the game, learning how to win victoriously, and how to lose graciously. I worked hard on my body—building it in the gym and through proper nutrition and sound personal habits and decisions. Most of all, I learned a lot about life—how to best prepare myself for the challenges I would face. I haven't always gotten it right, but I am more aware and better prepared because of the foundational lessons I learned and the principles I have applied since. Little did I realize, I was going through a transformation that I couldn't fully appreciate at the time.

The early days provided a foundation that has remained with me over the years. Since that time, I have been a student of success and achievement principles and philosophies, studying nearly everything I could get my hands on that had anything and everything to do with self-discovery, personal development, achievement, and success. Applying the principles to my life didn't always come easy. In fact, oftentimes I'd learned the hard way, discovering just as much from my failures and setbacks as my successes. Throughout it all I have learned to return to the basic principles that have consistently yielded the best results....

Create goals, write them down,
and act upon them.

From a Student to a Teacher

Although I can attest to the awesome power goal-setting had on my life, it wasn't until late in life that I discovered my full stride and decided it was time for me to give back. A successful author, speaker, mentor, and former college professor, I now dedicate my life to helping others see the value in achievement and success principles using the power of insight and awareness. I have assembled many years of collective wisdom to develop the concepts and philosophies you will find in this book. It is a gold mine of information that has worked for me and countless others, and it will work for you as well. In fact, it is the *gold mine* reference that inspired the title—GOAL MIND.

Your own GOAL MIND awaits. In the following pages, you will learn some of life's most important and powerful transformation concepts, philosophies, and strategies for achieving virtually *anything* you can imagine. The *only* limitations are those you place upon yourself. So, remove the limits of your imagination, push the boundaries of what you believe to be possible, and dare to achieve your own personal greatness!

Part One

∞

GOAL-SETTING

Chapter One

A Fresh New Perspective

"If you change the way you look at things, the things you look at change."
~ *Wayne Dyer*

What is it about successful people that sets them apart from everyone else? If you have ever wondered how *they* can achieve success with ease while others struggle or, worse yet, never seem to get anywhere, you're not alone. The simple fact is, most successful people are motivated by a goal-oriented mindset. They possess an intense desire to reach a goal or objective that they personally define as the essence of their success. Successful people know that the way to reach an objective is to set clear goals that support those objectives, and then they do something *every day* that takes them closer to their desired achievement.

Goal: /gōl/: an aspiration, an object or condition of
your desire to accomplish, achieve, or receive.

Your ability to achieve is based on a fundamental philosophy of effective goal-setting backed by action. Setting goals is an absolute essential element in the rituals you must establish in order to achieve any meaningful level of success. In fact, you have probably already experienced the benefits of this philosophy at some point in your life and may not fully realize it. Think about the last time you reached a goal or experienced a victory of some kind. It could have been a time when you saved enough for your first car or passed a difficult exam or landed your first job. Maybe it was the time you finally worked up the courage to introduce yourself to someone special in your life whom you had always wanted to meet. Chances are, you probably thought about it long and hard enough to establish some kind of plan, vision, or mental picture. In fact, it is in the *vision* that goals have their greatest power.

Vision is a source of energy and inspiration.

Here's the thing: most people have an aversion to goal-setting. They fail to acknowledge the powerful simplicity of the concept and begin to create excuses why they don't have the time, energy, circumstances, etc. to "waste" on setting goals. There are generally two schools of thought among these people. While one group believes they should be content with the way things are, the other group is constantly striving for more, and are never truly satisfied with what they have achieved. Both of these mindsets are ineffective because neither will produce the joy or happiness associated with achievement.

If you're not growing and changing, you're not happy. True happiness emanates from within. We are happiest when we are growing and improving. Therefore, the achievement of your goals should be such that you are fundamentally changed because of

4

them. Our conscious mind provides essential programming to our subconscious mind, which, in turn, ignites a source of energy that stimulates ideas leading to insight, inspiration, and the compelling emotional forces of change. Clearly defined goals transform desires from fleeting thoughts to inspiring possibilities. Careful contemplation of our goals leads to real and lasting change we read about, hear about, and witness in the lives of those enjoying the richness of this powerful philosophy. Isn't it time you joined them?

To be clear, a goal is *not* a strategy. A goal is a desire, coupled with an intent, to achieve something. The manner, practices, procedures, and strategies you will use to achieve your goals are not prerequisites for you to have a goal. In other words, you don't have to know *how* before you know *why*. Knowing why you want something is an absolute must and is a driving force to your ultimate goal achievement. In this chapter, you will learn the essential steps to successfully mapping the course to your personal gold mine. Knowing *why* you want something is the only prerequisite to getting started on these essential steps.

> ### *You don't have to know how before you know why.*

Never underestimate your ability to achieve your dreams and aspirations. You have more *ability* to achieve them than you most likely believe. In fact, your probability of success increases significantly when you use goals to reach your dreams and aspirations. Why then do so many people fall short of their true potential when it comes to attaining their dreams, goals, and objectives?

The key to attainment is in *the knowing*. For, if we do not know where it is we are going, or just what it is we desire, how will we ever develop a clear path to achievement, attainment, and success?

Herein lies the essence of effective goal-setting. Consider the following short story to support this mindset....

A State of Mind

Several years ago, on an extremely hot day, a crew of men were working on the roadbed of the railroad when they were interrupted by a slow-moving train. The train ground to a stop and a window in the last car—which incidentally was custom-made with air conditioning—was raised.

A booming, friendly voice called out, "Dave, is that you?" Dave Anderson, the crew chief called back, "Sure is, Jim, and it's really good to see you." With that pleasant exchange, Dave Anderson was invited to join Jim Murphy, the president of the railroad, for a visit. For over an hour, the men exchanged pleasantries and then shook hands warmly as the train pulled out.

Dave Anderson's crew immediately surrounded him as one of the men expressed astonishment that he knew Jim Murphy, the president of the railroad, as a personal friend. Dave then explained that twenty years earlier he and Jim Murphy had started to work for the railroad on the same day. One of the men, half-jokingly and half seriously asked Dave why he was still working out in the hot sun and Jim Murphy had gotten to be president. Rather wistfully Dave explained, "Twenty- three years ago, I went to work for $1.75 an hour and Jim Murphy went to work for the railroad."

Each of us is inherently programmed by a number of internal and external factors that form the basis of who we are and what we desire from life. We are as different and unique as each and every other human being on this earth, yet we have similarities that connect us to each other and to everything imaginable. In other words, each of us, as unique as we are, is an integral part of the entirety of life as we know it. This interconnectedness serves as a catalyst that provides powerful forces, which we can use to create individual experiences that form the basis of our dreams, goals, aspirations, and desires. We see and experience things physically, emotionally, spiritually, and intellectually because of the powerful nature of this concept. The enormity and existence of the concept is all too often misunderstood, taken for granted, or not considered at all. Why?

Most often, it is a mere lack of awareness that prevents us from seeing beyond a unilateral perspective where *we* are at the center of the universe. This "selfish" perspective *hinders* our ability to realize how *all* things exist as a vital part of each other and that we are but one aspect of the entirety.

Aside from the natural creations of God, everything you see around you began as an inspirational thought in the mind of someone. Manmade creations support the belief of our inherent tendency to not only survive but to *thrive* in a world where we must all coexist. It is the natural creations that remind us of the awe-inspiring nature of how we are all connected. These things serve to align us with the wonder of it all and remind us of the importance of focus and the absolute purity of a moment in time. It is there where we gain our greatest strength and inspiration for creativity. It is there where dreams, desires, and aspirations are born through the imaginative processes we all possess.

The creations of man, coupled with the natural creations that surround us, serve as influencing factors that form the basis of our desire for achievement. As we align the experiences of the external world with our internal minds and the wisdom we possess, we begin to discover our calling, our passions, and our desire to transform ourselves from who we are, to who we wish to become.

If you're the type of person who is still searching for your calling, rest assured, you're not alone. The fact that you are searching is encouraging because, whether you realize it or not, you are projecting an energy into the world that will bring you *exactly* what you seek. So...be careful what you ask for, because you will most certainly get it.

Before we get to the actual mechanics of setting and achieving goals, we should note that very few people reach their goals without first creating the conditions to receive that which they seek.

Focus

Your internal thoughts drive the perspective of how you perceive our external world. The lens from which you peer through is something you control. If you have ever used a pair of binoculars you know all too well that they require an adjustment of the lens to bring clarity to the objective. Your mind works in a similar fashion. You may not have a clear idea on the exact nature of your goals at first, but with a little patience and some focus of the lens of your introspection, you gain increasing clarity.

Do you truly believe you are capable of creating a goal so compelling that you will see it come to fruition? If so, you won't be surprised as you begin seeing your goal come into focus by employing the principles contained in this book. As your goal comes into focus, your ability to refine it, build it, and ultimately realize it is evidenced by the changes that take shape in your life, bringing you into alignment with achievement.

Most of our thought processes are driven, in large part, by two emotions: a desire to *gain* something or a desire to *protect* something. With every decision comes an internal evaluation of what the results of our decisions will bring to us or how it will protect us. We quickly evaluate whether acquiring something we desire is worth acting upon or avoiding altogether. The current position of our lives has largely been defined by the manner in which we generally approach these kinds of decisions and speaks to the mindset we have developed as a result of how we perceive things.

One of the most powerful tools we have as human beings is the power of choice. We can choose to see things positively or negatively. Are your goals positively defined, firmly rooted in a belief that you can indeed attain them? Or have you been taking a more cynical approach, choosing instead to focus more on the negative aspects of everyday issues and circumstance while blaming everyone and everything else for your current situation? The manner in which you frame your specific situation determines your focus and the likelihood of your outcome.

I have been a student of success philosophies most of my adult life. One of the most profound aspects I have discovered along my journey is the common traits that exist among successful people. Successful people are different, which is not to insinuate that their difference is unattainable by any stretch of the imagination. In fact, if we study these differences, we can use them as a template to create a foundation for our *own* successes. This book will provide several examples of the philosophies you can use as templates to form the basis of your own understanding as you begin to develop the skills you need to reach your personal goals.

The Powerful Nature of Goals

A clearly defined goal sets in motion forces beyond that which we fully understand, yet it is these forces that bring about the changes we desire. By simply deciding exactly what it is we want, powerful forces begin to take shape that bring us closer to our goal and our goal closer to us. It is a natural law of nature that provides an answer to every question, a reaction to every action, and a response to every effort. This law—often referred to as the Law of Reciprocity—provides us with an assurance that our goals will *always* be achieved, no matter the size or scope. It operates indiscriminately and, much like a computer, will bring you whatever you desire according to how you program it. CAUTION! *Every* goal includes those that are both good and not-so-good for us. So be careful how you define your goals and how you structure your programming.

Therefore, choose greatness over mediocrity. Choose change over chance. Use your personal power of choice to chart the course of your life and watch as the incredible nature of goals takes over and guides you directly to that which you desire.

> *"The major reason for setting a goal is for what it*
> *makes of you to accomplish it.*
> *What it makes of you will always be the far*
> *greater value than what you get."*
> ~ *Jim Rohn*

Goals give meaning to life. They direct energy toward the things we value. Setting goals provides us with long-term vision and short-term motivation. The process drives our ability to focus on our objectives and helps us to prioritize our time, money, and resources with efficiency. By setting sharp, clearly defined goals, we can measure our progress in what might have otherwise seemed like a long, arduous process.

So, if goal-setting is so powerful, why aren't more people setting goals? The reasons are as plentiful as you can imagine, yet they typically fall into two broad categories: awareness and fear. Fortunately, awareness can alleviate many fears associated with our ability to properly set (and eventually get) our goals.

Awareness

Most people are unaware of the powerful simplicity of goal-setting. They are unaware because, for the most part, goals were never a topic of discussion in the family or socialized within their peer groups. It is actually quite easy to see how someone with no exposure to the philosophy of goal-setting could reach adulthood without ever learning about goals. Theirs is simply a matter of education. Education leads to awareness. The more aware we are of our goals, the better we define them and consciously work toward them, the more likely we are to achieve them.

Awareness precedes our instinctive, curious nature. As we become aware of something new, our curiosity tends to inspire us to learn more. The more we learn about the *power* of setting goals, the more we discover about the *process*. Our ability to understand the process enables us to take the action steps necessary to see the *results* of this awesome power in our lives.

Sadly, most people don't create goals because, quite frankly, they honestly don't understand the process. Ask some people and they may *tell* you they have goals when, in reality, all they have are dreams or desires that are broadly defined by vague generalities. Answers such as, "I want to be happy," or "I want to be wealthy," or "I want a nice house" are more closely aligned with wishes, hopes, or dreams than they are with goals.

We all have dreams, desires, and wishes, but the clear difference between those who reach their dreams and those who don't, are defined by a thin veil of wisdom leading to the understanding of goals. Know this—your wishes and dreams will *not* materialize unless they are supported by a solid foundation of well-defined goals. On the contrary, your *goals* have the power to bring about the realization of your dreams and desires beyond your wildest expectations. Be careful to keep this in proper perspective to avoid frustration.

In order to be effective, goals must be clear, concise, and time-bound. Your goals must be *written* and easily measured. The test of a well-defined goal is one that can be described with passion and conviction to someone else and be easily understood. Power lies in the simplicity of a goal's construct. Your ability to design and shape such a goal is outlined in this book. I have purposely placed the bulk of that information in this first chapter to help you get started quickly. Knowing what to do and how to do it will change the entire journey of your life as your dreams begin to materialize through the *power* of your goals.

➢ **Clear** – A clearly-defined goal personalizes it in such a way that objectifies it and transforms it from something obscure to something you can begin to see as attainable. The more clarity you have with respect to your goals, the more potential you realize.

➢ **Concise** – A short but powerful way to describe your goal, serving to vividly remind you of its characteristics and the importance of its role in your life.

➢ **Time-bound** – A calendar deadline that compels you to act. A clearly-defined timeline does more for accomplishment than almost any other aspect of the goal-setting process. Meet your self-imposed deadlines and you will increasingly gain a sense of confidence that is unstoppable.

Desire

The start of any journey begins with a desire to travel. If we are to ever reach our destination or goal, it must be driven by a *desire* to reach a specific destination. Our desire *must* be strong enough to compel us to act and to compensate for the winds of change and circumstances we will inevitably encounter along the path of our journey. An intense burning desire assures us that we will have the fortitude and stamina to overcome any and all obstacles that may come between us and our goal. In other words, we must show up and be ready to do whatever it takes to achieve our goal despite the obstacles and inevitable distractions of life.

The pursuit of goals enables us to release our full potential for personal and professional achievement and success. In setting goals, we find purpose, growth, opportunity, and achievement, not to mention the ultimate reward—happiness through a balanced and purpose-driven life.

Effective Navigation

The importance of navigation cannot be overstated when it comes to setting goals. You *must* know where you are going before you set out to achieve your goals. In fact, your goal is the defining essence of your destination. As a former air traffic controller, I have seen the benefits of effective navigation at its finest. In the air—as in life—there are no street signs. However, there *are* principles of navigation that—if learned, understood, and practiced—can take you anywhere you desire to go. I can tell you with absolute certainty that the skies above us would be nowhere near as safe without these principles of navigation in place. The same holds true for the destinations of our goals and aspirations.

Get into the Zone

Before we begin the navigation process, let's take a moment to consider just where we are in terms of how ready we are to travel. We'll do this by conducting a quick but honest self-assessment with the easy-to-reference Achievement Zone map below.

As you'll see from the map, there are four zones, each describing an ideal progression of personal growth from the safe and familiar *Comfort Zone* to a zone we all aspire to experience—the *Growth Zone*. To gain the most from this map, take a look at each zone to determine your current state of mind with respect to where you believe you currently reside when it comes to achieving your goal.

It's worth mentioning that most people tend to reside in the first or second zones, especially at first. It's a natural human tendency to seek comfort and familiarity within the confines of the **Comfort Zone**. Anything outside this zone is an area of vulnerability where doubt pervades and self-confidence is typically at its lowest.

The Comfort Zone is one of the toughest to escape because it borders the dreaded **Fear Zone**. This zone exists largely because of the power we give it. Our willingness to give fear its power keeps us anchored to the zone where we feel safest. Instead of pushing past our fears to discover and experience life-changing breakthroughs, we very often retreat to the sanctity of the familiar comfort zone. The key to getting past both of these zones as quickly as possible is to establish *clarity, courage, conviction*, and *commitment*.

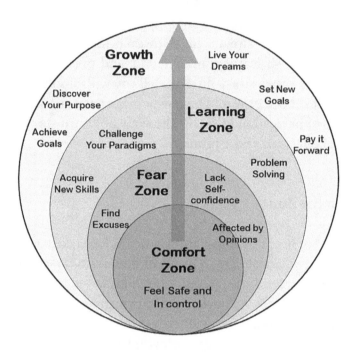

The Achievement Zone

Clarity

Of all the things that prevent us from reaching our biggest goals and tasting the true essence of success, *fear* is our biggest nemesis. We tend to fear the unknown. When we establish a new goal, we are, in essence, declaring a desired outcome of the results we hope to achieve. It's at this point where we have the highest expectations but the least amount of information and tools on just how the heck we're going to achieve our goal. So, how do we effectively arm ourselves for success? By establishing a crystal clear and compelling vision of our goal.

Courage

What was it that drove you to create your goal? What were the conditions? What is the story? WHY did you create this goal? Do you want this goal so badly that you are willing to do whatever it takes to achieve it? Answer these questions and others like them and you will have the foundation necessary to drive through any obstacle, including almost anything the Fear Zone poses.

Conviction

Our convictions are deeply connected to the values by which we live. Our values drive everything from the daily decisions we make to the spiritual beliefs we hold dear. The fundamental basis of our goals should rest upon the things we value. If they do not, we'll never get past the Fear Zone, where doubt and uncertainty will easily convince us not to waste the time and effort. It's easy to disrupt a plan that is loosely based on hope and desire. But a plan based on conviction brings with it an attitude of alignment we can wear as a coat of armor when challenges arise.

Commitment

Your resolve to persevere against inevitable obstacles and challenges is a difference-maker in the goal achievement process. Commitment is the cornerstone of consistency—a practice that produces measurable results. Consistency opens the door to physical, emotional, and cognitive development. Your ability to stay committed to your goal assures you will develop new skills and insight others will see as unique and gifted.

You will have greater power over the elements and conditions that exist in the Fear Zone as you gain confidence through clarity, courage, conviction, and commitment. Your growth and development will lead you to the **Learning Zone**—an area where some of your biggest breakthroughs will occur. You will see things differently, challenge traditional viewpoints and perspectives, acquire new skills, and begin to realize the results of your efforts. Those who make it to this zone are, by far, more likely to achieve the goals they have set for themselves.

I often used to wonder why the people who seemed to have it all were able to do so much and be so happy doing it. I envied them. What made them so special? It took me a long time to learn that almost all of them had to take the same path through the Achievement Zone to get where they were. I no longer envy them. Instead, I admire them. And I follow the principles and philosophies they used to find their way to the **Growth Zone**. The Growth Zone is where you realize the true value of the journey. Your arrival to this zone gives you a unique perspective on the goal achievement process unlike any other. This zone offers the rewards of achievement as well as new opportunities to continue to grow, give back, or pay forward. It is a zone that allows you to discover the essence of achievement—the ability to truly know yourself.

One Degree

When it comes to direction or a course of travel, one degree can make a profound difference and determine whether we reach our goal or miss it altogether. In aviation, a one-degree difference in an assigned heading or compass course trajectory can cause an aircraft to stray miles off course, preventing it from ever reaching its intended destination. It is an analogy I use all the time to demonstrate the importance of maintaining focus on the goal and to continually monitor progress along the path to achievement.

We simply cannot take an ad hoc approach to life without realizing, sooner or later, that it will take us places we have no intention or desire to go if we are disengaged and distracted. This approach leads only to frustration and unhappiness. Sadly, it is an approach taken by far too many people as they philosophically "take one day at time" or yield to the circumstances of life, believing they have little choice but to accept things as they occur. These are the same people who, after many years of living life without a goal or plan, find themselves broke, unhappy in their job, in dissatisfying relationships, and making little progress in life. These are the people who choose to repeat the same habits and rituals they have become accustomed to that keep them trapped in a lifestyle they despise.

Goals provide us with a sense of purpose and direction. These attributes add value to our lives and lead to fulfillment and happiness. As we make strides toward our goals, we feel empowered, vital, competent, confident, and happy. Every step we take toward our goals leads to a belief that we can achieve that which we set out to accomplish. Our achievement leads to growth and the knowledge that we are capable, so we set higher goals and continue our quest to grow, to contribute, and to find happiness and fulfillment—all of which you will find in the Growth Zone.

Let's Navigate...

The navigation process requires careful thought and consideration of things we must do in order to reach our goal. The two primary requirements of navigation are *action* and *analysis*. In other words, we must *analyze* the *actions* we must take in order to reach our objective. And then we must consistently follow through with action.

A fundamental requirement of navigation is to determine a destination. With that in mind, select your destination (goal), and let's go from where you are (starting point) to where you desire to be over the course of time. Consider the following steps to map the course to *your* personal goals.

Step 1: Choose a Destination (Goal)

Before you begin your journey, it is always a good idea to know where you are going. Goal-setting is no different. Goal navigation requires us to have more than a "pretty good idea" on where we're headed, so take some time with this.

So, where are you right now? While most of us have a *pretty good* idea of where we are in terms of knowledge and resources, it is always a good idea to measure the talents, gifts, and resources we already have against the skills we need to develop in order to generate increasing resources to foster the momentum we need for growth and goal attainment.

Analysis: Once you have a good idea on where you are, start thinking about the roles you want to assume or relationships you want to establish—such as becoming a better spouse, supervisor, leader, manager, mentor, or business owner—and identify those. Visualize yourself stepping into these new roles. Set yourself up for success. Make your goal challenging but attainable. Determine your *existing* roles and relationships with respect to personal and professional categories (spouse, parent, friend, hobbyist, volunteer, writer, speaker, etc.).

Action: Write a brief statement describing each role you intend to occupy and how you see yourself in the role. How will the role affect your life and the lives of others? Describe it. Write it down as if it has already materialized. This present tense context shifts our subconscious minds into accepting the new role and opens the pathways to change.

Example: I am a better parent because of my new level of physical fitness. I am now able to actively participate with my spouse and children in virtually any activity—physical, mental, or emotional. I am healthy and alert. My family can tell the difference in my outlook on life, and we are closer because of it.

Develop some objectives for each statement that provides a pathway for meeting both the existing and anticipated visions you have for each role or relationship. Adjust the narrative of your statements as you make progress.

Example: Lose twenty-five pounds by [specific date]. Walk two miles daily. Increase lean muscle mass by 5% by [date].

Step 2: Map Your Goals

Mapping is a critical process that allows us to plan the details of our journey. I often use the analogy of a pilot who plans a route of flight to a specific destination, taking into account every variable that will or may occur along the journey—speed, altitude, weather, other traffic, etc. The same holds true for the elements of life we must also consider when planning to navigate to our goals.

Analysis: Determine the goals you want to accomplish for each role or relationship you desire. Be mindful to maintain an appropriate balance between roles while you create your personal map. The point here is to ensure you don't overwhelm yourself with an unrealistic plan of achievement. Imbalance will derail your efforts, so be mindful of this as you go through the process. Consider the obstacles you may encounter and do your best to plan for them. Will you require more knowledge, money, or assistance before you get underway?

Action: List your goals on a whiteboard or other medium. Use a large enough "space" (whatever the medium) to create a map that connects your overall objective (your goal) with the steps you must take to get there. Connect the elements on your list with something you can clearly visualize. If you are so inclined—or you're a visually-minded person, as I am—make it fun by using map symbols or elements. Using something like the goal map example at the end of this chapter is a great way to track your progress.

Ensure each goal is truly aligned with who you are (your talents, abilities, values, intentions, and passions). If it is not, consider other alternatives.

Step 3: Evaluate Your Goals

Action: For each goal, determine a start date and a deadline. Place these dates on a calendar where you can see them every single day. Even if you do not know *how* the goal is going to be achieved, always give yourself a firm deadline. You'll be amazed at the progress you do make when you conduct an objective evaluation of your progress.

Action: Measure your progress. Create intermediate "check points" or milestones. Be sure to include these on your goal map. Use the check points to determine whether you are on pace to meet your desired deadline. If so, great! If not, reevaluate, reassess, and adjust your deadline and your plan accordingly. Don't beat yourself up if you're not where you want to be in terms of meeting the timeline. The true essence of success is the *steady progress* toward your goals. So, if you're making progress, keep going and adjust when necessary. Use the color-coded (or shaded) quadrant progress tool depicted on the goal map example at the end of this chapter as an indicator of your accomplishments.

Analysis: Evaluate the resources required to accomplish your goals as well as the expected rewards or benefits of achievement. You will undoubtedly require time, money, or education at a minimum, so be prepared to invest in your goals. You will learn soon enough that an investment in your goals is an investment in yourself that always provides a great rate of return.

Evaluate the obstacles. An effective evaluation of the predictable obstacles prepares you with a solutions mindset. More on this in a later chapter.

Action: Write a description of the results of achieving your goal. A clear "results statement" helps crystallize the end state of what you aspire to achieve. It also reaffirms your WHY and serves as a great inspirational narrative to drive your momentum.

Action: Express your commitment to the goal with written affirmations and declarations: positive motivational statements written in present or future tense that declare why and how you'll accomplish the goal. Don't overlook this part of the process, as it is a powerful force multiplier that will bolster your ability to connect with the reasons you are pursuing your goal in the first place.

Step 4: Create Your Action Plan

Analysis: Brainstorm the objectives, actions, and activities required to accomplish your goal. What do you need to do first, second, and so forth? Go back to your map as you consider the incremental steps you must take to get started. Come up with several ways or "routes" to your goal. This strategy will help you see around the inevitable obstacles that are likely to emerge along the path to goal achievement.

Action: Set specific milestone objectives. Establish realistic, but challenging, deadlines for each milestone.

Analysis and Action: Determine the most effective action or activity to accomplish each objective and do *that* first.

Step 5: Implement Your Plan

"Implementation" is just a fancy word for *action.* So, get going… do something…*act!* You can have the best plan, the best reasons, intentions, and desires, but if you don't back it up with action, you will go nowhere fast.

Action: Commit and schedule time to perform each goal-related activity every single day. Inconsistency will KILL your goal attainment strategy. Therefore, do something <u>every single day</u> to bring your goals closer to fruition. READ something related to your goal.

21

DO something related to your goal. INVEST in something related to your goal. If you're not getting closer to your goal, there is *always* a reason. Most of time that reason is based on inconsistency or inaction, which is something you can clearly control.

Here are your keys...*now soar!*

The very act of *thinking* about our goals makes us happy by giving us hope. With this in mind, we should make it a daily habit to review our goals. Write down your goals and put them in places where you are exposed to them every day. Habits like this help to develop a laser-like focus that ultimately drives the way we think and communicate as we pursue our goals. Decide, from this moment on, to be *a goal-seeking machine*, moving with precision toward the things you have determined to be important. You will not only reach your goals, but you will also find happiness as you pursue them.

Never forget, *you* are in the driver's seat of your life. You are in full control of how you react to everything you will encounter. You must get behind the wheel in the right state of mind, bring a steady focus, and prepare for the circumstances that will invariably surface along your journey. You must remain alert and aware while not allowing fear to disrupt or distract your navigation skills nor your desire to reach your destination. You *can* do it!

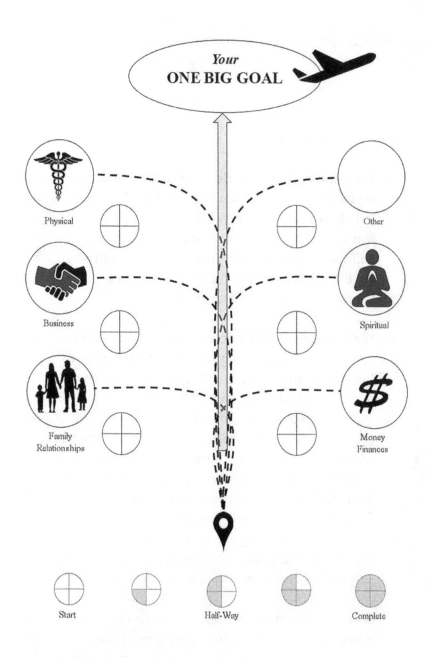

A good plan is like a roadmap: it shows the final destination and reveals the best way to get there.
~ H. Stanley Judd

Some Final Thoughts

- ➤ **Choose a destination. Begin with the end in mind.** Visualize the utopia that defines your ideal life. Use your five senses to help you to shape it. What does it look like? What does it feel like? What are the new sensations and experiences that will likely materialize by reaching your destination? These are the fundamental elements of a worthy goal whether it is your desired lifestyle or *any* goal.

- ➤ **Write it down!** Write down the details of what you experience as you bring your goals to the forefront of your mind. Put them someplace you will see them every day. Write your own story. And never ever give up on the objective to meet your expectations. Far too many people have given up on their goals because of circumstances. Remember, circumstances do not define us (or our goals). We are more accurately defined by our resolve to overcome circumstance to reach our desired objectives. Circumstance is just another moniker fear uses to disguise itself and disrupt our focus. Don't allow circumstance to change or get in the way of your goals. Only *you* should change or adjust your goals, and only because you desire to, not because circumstance dictates.

- ➤ **Own your goal.** Claiming ownership of your goal seems simple enough, but far too many people choose erroneous goals based on the expectations or influence of others. Don't get me wrong; there are other people in our lives we must consider—our immediate family, for example—but even they should respect the fact that *you* are part of the overall vision of your collective destination. Once you own your goal, pursue it with passion. The simple truth is you will likely fall short of reaching your goal if you do not create a *burning desire* to achieve it. Life will throw a great many obstacles or circumstances into your path along the way. Without a burning desire to reach your goals, overcoming those obstacles will seem insurmountable and somehow not worth the fight. Your reasons to *refrain* from taking action will overpower your reasons *for* taking the actions necessary to adapt and overcome. Don't allow that to happen.

➢ **Nurture your goal.** There is nothing more motivating than seeing your goal begin to materialize. An overwhelming confidence begins to emerge as you see some of the elements of your plan take shape (think *Learning Zone*). Confidence quiets fear and instills a conviction fear despises. Be mindful that you must continue to nurture your goal with the care and feeding it requires. You must continually watch over it and proactively guard against all of fear's tactics that are designed to prevent you from realizing your objectives. You *must* keep your burning desire alive and do whatever it takes to reach your goal.

Thought-provoking questions...

1. What are your goals? Are they truly aligned with your desires?

2. What activities bring out the passions and greatest sense of purpose in your life? Focus on that.

3. Your perception is not absolute. You can change it by getting out of your own way. What changes can you make *right now* that will allow you to see things from a different perspective? (Think habits and rituals.)

Chapter Two

Return on Investment

"The secret of success is making your vocation your vacation."
~ Mark Twain

If we are to achieve anything at all we must get beyond hope. We must determine whether we are merely *interested* or *committed* to achievement. Along with this mindset, we must consider the ROI or *return on investment* as it applies to the efforts we make to achieve our goals.

There is a distinct difference between interest and commitment when it comes to the pursuit of our goals. The significance lies in the amount of work it will take and the amount of effort we are willing to make to achieve our goals. If we are *interested* in achieving our goal then we will do *only* what is convenient and, if things work out well, then we are generally satisfied. If, on the other hand, the tasks become arduous or overwhelming, we will easily find and express reasons and excuses to compensate for our underachievement.

A commitment, on the other hand, is a difference-maker in terms of the things we will do in order to achieve our goals. Quite frankly, if we are committed, we will do whatever it takes to achieve our goals. We will learn, grow, plan, invest in ourselves, and take action, starting right now, and follow up with consistency (daily, weekly, monthly, etc.). We will do whatever it takes to create a new life supported by new rituals that immediately place us into alignment with our goals. We will discover the energy and the willingness to do something every day that will bring us closer to our goals, and we will not allow anything to disrupt the flow to achievement.

Commitment will change you. It will transform you from who you are to who you wish to become. Your awareness will increase in such a way that you will notice when you must make small corrections or adjustments, and you will do it faster and better than anyone else who is merely *interested* in achieving their goals. This is the clear difference between those who achieve and those who don't.

The achiever realizes a return on investment that far exceeds the initial efforts they make to attain their goals. Their returns are often measured in multiple ways: psychologically, monetarily, emotionally, spiritually, and physically.

I had always wanted to be a mentor to young people. So, naturally, I set a goal to become a mentor and got busy preparing myself over the years in an effort to put myself in a position to serve when the opportunity presented itself. One of the earliest mentoring experiences I had is also among the most memorable and rewarding in terms of a return on investment. While my hope was to provide a benefit for the young man I initially mentored, it turns out the benefit was mutual. The value we provided to each other over the years still exists to this day as we travel the individual paths of our lives, connecting from time to time, sharing our insight, experiences, philosophies, and victories with each other from wherever we are in life. This experience for me has repeated itself many times over with as many people in various walks of life. It has far exceeded any return on investment that I could have imagined.

When it comes to goals, there are two overarching but vitally important aspects: *setting* them and *getting* them.

Setting Goals

It goes without saying that most anyone can *set* a goal. Believe it or not, however, there are actually some people who *never* set goals, at least not consciously. The Bible tells us that a man without a vision shall perish. It is largely believed that most everyone has a general idea of what they desire in their life, even for the most carefree among us. That's not to say, however, that everyone knows the fundamentals of how to actually set a goal.

If your desire is to have a role in shaping the circumstances of your life, you should know how to properly set goals. Setting goals accomplishes two main objectives: it provides a long-term vision and short-term motivation. Your long-term vision enhances the focus of your objective or goal. In other words, it provides clarity in terms of exactly what you desire as an end state.

Setting your goal requires you to describe it. As you do, be sure to think about the many ways it personally resonates with your WHY—the reasons you desire the goal. The best way to do that is to set goals that follow the SMART methodology.

SMART Goals

A useful way of making goals more powerful is to use the SMART mnemonic. Now, this is not a new concept, but it is one worth mentioning because it has stood the test of time, and it works. While there are plenty of variants (some of which are included in parenthesis), SMART usually stands for:

> ➤ **S – Specific** (or Significant)
> ➤ **M – Measurable** (or Meaningful)
> ➤ **A – Attainable** (or Action-Oriented)
> ➤ **R – Relevant** (or Rewarding)
> ➤ **T – Time-bound** (or Trackable)

For example, instead of setting a goal "to run a full marathon," it is more effective to use the SMART goal concept "to have completed my first marathon by [a specific date]." The specificity of this goal sets you up for success with the proper mindset that will systematically begin to go to work *for* you instead of *against* you. You will begin to understand—with increasing clarity—the steps required to achieve your goal because of using this SMART construct.

Specific – Define your goal with an accurate description of what it should look like. The more details the better. How will it make you feel once it materializes? How will it affect your life or the lives of others? What are the quantities, colors, and attributes of your goal? Specificity goes a long way in bringing about the achievement of goals. Don't neglect this vital first step in the process, or you will be behind from the very start.

Measurable – Establish concrete criteria for measuring the progress of your goal. Measuring your progress helps assure that you remain on track, reach your target dates, and experience the thrill of achievement that compels you to continue past inevitable roadblocks and distractions. To determine whether your goal is measurable, ask questions such as how much, how many, and how will I know it is complete? A note of advice—be careful of measuring your progress with money. Money is a by-product of your success.

Attainable – You can attain most any goal you set when you create your initial plan and establish a timeframe that supports your plan of action. Goals that may at first seem unattainable seem closer, not because they become any easier, but because *you* find ways to grow and achieve them. When you write down your goals, they become tangible (even if merely on paper). Tangible goals become attainable goals because you begin to see yourself in relation to the goals and set the groundwork for developing the traits, personality, and skills that allow you to possess them.

Realistic – Every goal you set should present an objective for which you personally are both *willing* and *able* to work. Realistic goals provide an inherent incentive toward progress. If you set unrealistic goals, you will eventually give up on them and quit.

Realistic goals paint a picture that resonates so deep within the core of your WHY that you will stop at nothing to achieve them.

Timely – Every goal should have an associated timeline of completion. A timeline creates a sense of urgency and goes a long way toward convincing the subconscious mind to do everything it can to meet the suspense date. When setting a timeline, keep in mind the realistic step just before this one. Unrealistic timelines cause frustration and only serve to sabotage goals. Although most of us want to achieve our goals in as little time as possible, we are wise to keep in mind that a realistic timeline reinforces the likelihood of accomplishment because we develop a belief that the goal will likely be achieved in a sensible timeframe.

Here are some more guidelines that will help you set effective, achievable goals:

➤ **Write down your goals** – Writing your goals down crystallizes them, makes them tangible, and convinces the subconscious that you are serious. What our eyes see our mind believes. The subconscious mind cannot distinguish between what is real and what is not. Writing your goals is one way of convincing your subconscious mind that something exists even before it has materialized.

➤ **Be positive** – Cast your goals in a positive light. Don't describe them as a problem. Instead, describe them as a project. This subtle technique will help to convince your subconscious that your goal is attainable and will also be a pleasurable journey instead of an arduous task.

➤ **Be specific** – Set precise goals. Include dates, times, milestones, and outcomes so that you can measure your achievement. This approach allows you to know exactly where you are on the path to achievement and leaves no doubt as to when you have achieved your goal. Specificity also feeds your motivation, as it provides real feedback in terms of progress. After all, the more progress you experience the more motivated you become. Be sure to describe your goal in great detail. What does it look like? What does it sound like, taste like, etc.? Consider all of the five senses as you describe it, then go *one* step further and visualize the *experience* of having achieved your goal. Oftentimes, an intrinsic motivator is *far* more powerful than any other external force.

➢ **Set priorities** – *Action* is required to achieve every goal. But what should we do first, second, third, and so on? Setting your task or action priorities helps you to avoid feeling overwhelmed and directs your attention to the most important and most effective steps to take on first.

➢ **Don't bite off more than you can chew** – Divide your goals into challenging but manageable units that you can control. Big goals are okay, but if your interim goals are too large and unmanageable, it can lead to frustration, distraction, and defeat. Keeping goals manageable leads to empowerment, confidence, and systematically enhances the chances of a successful outcome.

In the previous chapter, I described how I had often wondered what made the difference between those who are successful and those who are not. I explained that whether we achieve success to any great degree depends largely upon three basic principles I call the Triple-S: our Strategy, our Story, and our State.

While having a sound strategy is indeed a wise thing, it should be noted that strategies by themselves don't change lives—implementation does. Most people don't implement effectively (or at all) because their story (personal narrative) doesn't support action. And, until it does, their conditions will never truly change.

I'm sure you've heard some of the more common story narratives before:

"I've tried everything, and it just won't work."
"That only happens in the movies."
"You have to *have* money to make money."
"I just don't have time for..."

You should divorce these story narratives at once! Instead, find someone who has achieved what you wish to achieve and change your story using *their* formula for success until you develop your own. Find out what *they* believe and then, adopt a similar, but uniquely personal mindset. I think you'll find that it's refreshingly different from what you may currently believe. The perspective alone can *catapult* your momentum, not to mention your results.

Your Story

My youngest granddaughter loves to hear me tell stories. The wondrous expressions on her face reveals a total immersion; her mind is a wellspring of imagination as she listens intently to the things I make up on the fly.

Dragons and princesses, mermaids, and pirates abound as we journey through the wonder of our vivid imaginations together. We can literally go anyplace we desire inside the narrative of a story. As adults, we have the same freedoms when it comes to using our imaginations. Unfortunately, most people underestimate the power they have to change the narrative they have adopted.

"Imagination is more important than knowledge.
For knowledge is limited to all we know and
understand, while imagination embraces the entire
world and all there ever will be to understand."
~ Albert Einstein

Our story defines the way we look at life. We form the narrative through the lens of our experiences as well as the outside influences we allow to feed our imaginations and biases. If our experiences contain the elements of hope, opportunity, and possibility, then the basis of our story is built upon the foundation of those precepts.

Very often, those who have achieved success have experienced a breakthrough of sorts. When we hear this, it resonates because that seems to be exactly what we're looking for: a breakthrough that will lead us to the holy grail of success and achievement. Our quest, however, begs the question of exactly what sort of breakthrough we're looking for.

Each of us has a personal narrative—a story—that we *consistently* tell ourselves we must fulfill in order to have an ideal life leading to happiness. As we become more conscious of our personal story, we acquire the wisdom to make adjustments in our life that help us to match our lives with the narrative of our story and the nature of our desires. For example, we may believe that an ideal life is defined by going to college, graduating, landing a great job, finding the perfect mate, living in a specific home in a specific neighborhood, having and raising x-number of children, and living happily ever after.

Your story is likely different from the one just described, especially given the multitude of options and differences in ideals we all have. But one thing has remained the same—many people believe that in order for life to matter, they must achieve a great deal for life to equate to happiness. That couldn't be further from the truth.

Far too many of us have been conditioned to connect the elements (people, places, job, circumstances, etc.) and the progress of our story to the effect it has on our happiness. That's all well and good until our lives don't align with the story we have written or envisioned.

The way each of us frames reality is diverse and unique. We interpret our experiences through the lens of our psychology, which forms the basis of our story. Everything matters—from the history of our experiences to our gender, external influences, and cultural differences. We form attitudes, opinions, and hopes that shape what we consider to be realistic, morally acceptable, and noteworthy. We predicate our goals and ideals upon these elements and systematically use them to write our story.

Think about a time or circumstance where you were absolutely happy, joyous, or thrilled with life. Chances are it was because your circumstances met or exceeded the story narrative you have with that aspect of your life.

Now think of a time or circumstance where you were absolutely miserable. Can you guess why you were miserable? My bet is that you can associate it to something centered upon or around your circumstances at the time.

When your conditions don't match the story you have written for your life, you will have pain and discontent. When this occurs, there are three choices you can make.

1. Blame something or someone else.

2. Change your story.

3. Change your life.

Blaming something or someone has little utility beyond the satisfaction of a temporary and regrettable reaction to an outlet you'd be best advised to avoid. There is no personal growth potential or benefit whatsoever with this misguided approach.

The latter two options have some viability when you consider that you may, in fact, be unable or unwilling to meet the ideal of what you have adopted as the story you have written for your life. If this is the case, then perhaps it's time to change your story. In other words, a shift in the way you see your life may be in order. There's no shame in taking this approach because, as I have stated, happiness is personally defined by a congruence of our life with our story. Changing that story is one approach to realigning our story to better match our life and bring harmony to the forefront.

On the other hand, if you know there are areas of your life that you have the power and willingness to change in order to meet the narrative of your story, then you should do precisely that—change your life. Doing so will empower you and re-shape the conditions and circumstances that begin to meet your story. So, what are some of the ways you can change your life to meet or *exceed* the story narrative you have written?

One alternative to consider is to change some of your story and *some* of your life to find the happiness and contentment you seek. This hybrid approach is often referred to as "an adjustment" that many people make as they grow in knowledge and wisdom in their pursuit of success and happiness. Quite often, all it takes is an adjustment to begin seeing the changes you seek to realign your story and begin an experience of happiness and contentment. As the experiences of your life lead you toward the narrative of your story, your ideal success will be "naturally" attracted to you.

What about you? What's your story? Does your story support the life you're leading? If so, great! If not, why not? What can you do to change things?

Enjoy the Victory

Once your story is aligned with your strategy, you'll be in a position to begin to see real progress with your goals. As you reach each goal, be sure to take the time to immerse yourself in the satisfaction of your achievement. Savor the moment as you look back upon the steps you took to get where you are as well as the changes you've observed in yourself through the accomplishment of your goal. Also, take note of the progress you've made toward other goals in the achievement of this specific goal. What have you learned that will help you craft and achieve your *next* goal?

Rewarding yourself appropriately for your achievement reinforces the habits and rituals you formed on your journey to achievement. It also helps breed self-confidence and the assurance that you can continue to achieve any goal you set.

Now would be a great time to review other goals you have on the drawing board:

> If you achieved your most recent goal easily, set your next goal a bit higher.

> If the goal consumed too much time and resources, consider a reevaluation while keeping in mind all of the lessons you learned by achieving this goal. Perhaps you can lay in more milestones that will help better indicate your progress to serve as motivators along the way to your next goal.

> If you recognize the need to improve your personal skills, set a goal to acquire the knowledge and expertise to complete your next set of goals. Then take action to do just that. Action is the precursor of results.

Key Points

Goal-setting is an important way to:

> Decide what you want to achieve in life

> Separate what's important from what's irrelevant

> Motivate yourself

> Build your self-confidence, self-esteem, and self-awareness

Set your Grand Goals first. Then, set a three-to-five-year plan of milestone goals that you need to complete if you are to reach your lifetime Grand Goal. Keep the process moving by regularly reviewing and adjusting your goals as you meet or exceed them. And remember to take time to enjoy the satisfaction of achieving your goals as you complete them.

If you don't already set goals, why not begin right now? As you make this a part of your life, you'll find your career accelerating, your life improving, and your happiness soaring, all the while wondering just how you ever functioned beforehand.

Some Final Thoughts

➢ **Set your goal.** The importance of setting goals provides a long-term vision and short-term motivation. Your long-term vision enhances the focus of your objective or goal and helps to determine the extent to which you can operate effectively toward your goal. Each incremental move toward your goal is cumulative. In other words, results breed consistency and tenacity—two essential elements of goal achievement.

➢ **Determine your WHY.** Knowing your WHY—the reasons you desire the goal—helps determine the level of commitment you have for the accomplishment of your goal. It is also a pre-indication of the amount of action you are willing to expend in order to achieve your objective. A *burning desire* is one that will help you get past inevitable obstacles and temptations.

➢ **Be SMART.** Remember to use the SMART mnemonic to help you in crafting your goals. This SMART approach provides the foundation upon which all goals are realized and is one you can easily recall as you build your plan for success.

➢ **Write your own story.** Your story is the essence of WHY you do the things you do. No matter what efforts you make, you will always realign yourself with the storyline you have created for yourself. If you strive to achieve a goal or objective that is misaligned with your story, frustration will inevitably come about sooner or later. Our legacy anchors us to our past. In order to reach "new" goals, we must let go of the past and create a new storyline that matches the objectives we intend to achieve from hence forward.

Thought-provoking questions...

1. Take a few moments, once again, to reflect upon your goals. Are you *interested* or are you *committed* to achieving them? If you are not committed, you should take the time to reconsider whether the goal is worth pursuing at all in the first place.

2. Have you remembered to use the SMART mnemonic as a guide when setting your goal? While doing so does not guarantee its accomplishment, it is a clear advantage to do so when considering the success rate it typifies in the goal-setting process.

3. Have you written down your goals in such a way as to cast it in a positive manner? Were you specific in your description? Did you connect your goal to all five senses while being sure to remember to visualize the experience of your achievement? Have you placed your goal on the calendar in order to set an expected completion date? Have you set your priorities and done your best to eliminate distractions?

Chapter Three

A Clean Slate

> *"We all start at zero. We all start at the beginning. Don't give up."*
> *~ Anonymous*

Life is a numbers game. Everyone starts at zero. The faster you realize that, the better off you'll be in terms of understanding how the success and goal achievement process works. The goal achievement process takes work. It also takes an understanding that some people will reach their achievements faster than others. Like I said, it's a numbers game.

The defining factor in any achievement process is *work*. You don't have to be smart, but it helps. More people have achieved success because they were willing to work harder and longer than most other people who have a better idea than they do. Work ethic is the *number one* factor that separates the achievers from the dreamers.

When you begin setting your goals, part of your strategy should be to conduct an initial evaluation of where you've been, where you are, and where you intend to go. This is the baseline by which you will draw all measurements. Your initial assessment will show you exactly where your *clean slate* is in terms of a starting point. Be honest with yourself. Don't over- or under-estimate anything, most especially your ability to step up to the challenge of what it will take to achieve your goals. If it's knowledge you require, there are educational sources you can tap into that will help you. If it's people you need, there are ways for you to collaborate and gain the trust and attention of the right people to influence your progress. Every answer is available to everyone. Some answers just require a bit more work to uncover.

> *"Your objective is to bridge the gap between where you are now and the goals you intend to reach."*
> ~ *Earl Nightingale*

Is your goal realistic, based on where you are today and the timeline you have given yourself to reach it? If your goal is not realistic, force yourself to be *completely* honest and revise both your calculations and your projections. If you don't, you will only be met with frustration and disappointment. Keep your heart set upon the goal and your mind set upon the process to get there. The strategy will emerge if you do the work required to find it.

Practice Clean-Slate Thinking

One of the most valuable exercises you can engage in as you begin to plan your goal attainment strategy is "clean-slate" thinking. In clean-slate thinking, you assume nothing except for the fact that you know only what you know and nothing more. You are essentially willing to start with a *clean slate*.

With every initiative comes a starting point. Recall when you were in school, how the teacher would start with a clean slate (or chalkboard or whiteboard) to begin a new lesson. This clean slate concept does not assume you know *nothing* but rather takes into account what you *do* know in the form of preconceptions, and sets it aside temporarily, allowing room for you to consider new concepts from a fundamental baseline of knowledge. The zero-baseline strategy places you squarely on the ground floor in terms of the things you need to learn to begin your goal achievement process. It's amazing what you will discover if you will accept the fact that you don't know everything and are willing to learn a new process with an open mind.

You may find that you should apply clean-slate thinking to the people in your life as well—both from a business and personal standpoint. Some of the wealthiest people I know surround themselves with others who share similar philosophies, ideals, and ideas. The quality of your relationships is critical to helping you reach your goals. Are there relationships in *your* life you need to eliminate or redefine? Are there new relationships you need to seek and cultivate? Start with a clean slate to consider the kinds of relationships *you* need to reach your goals.

With the clean slate concept in mind, examine every aspect of your work experience, career, hobbies, and interests. Are you adept at any particular skillset? Do you currently provide a service similar to that which you intend to bring to more people? If so, remember to think big and keep in mind the many ways you can use your strengths to enhance the service you intend to bring to the masses. Start with a clean slate to strategize the elements you need to accelerate your momentum.

Practical exercise: Start with a clean slate—*literally*.

1. Purchase or acquire a white board (clean slate) that you can use to begin brainstorming.

2. Put a marker in your hand and step back a few paces from the whiteboard. The marker in your hand is important because it drives intent—the intent to create. Holding the marker convinces your subconscious mind that you are prepared to write something, so it effectively opens the door to everything that is possible—answers, ideas, and insight—when they come to you. You would be surprised at how powerful this one simple strategy can be.

3. Stare at the blank slate as you focus on your goal. Allow the elements of your goal to fill your mind.

4. Time to write! Begin with a description of your goal. Write everything that comes to mind. Now is not the time to be obsessive about being organized. Just write. What does it look like? Where are you when your goal materializes? Who are you with? What do you feel, smell, taste, and hear?

5. Ask yourself what action you need to take to get started on your goal. Write the first thing that comes to mind. Prioritize the action steps only when you have written all you can think of.

6. Analyze your gap-fillers. Where are your biggest knowledge gaps? Do you lack funding? Will your strategy attract investors? What sources can best address the deficiencies you identify? What are your associated risks versus the rewards you expect? Is there anything you can hire others to do while you focus on the main tasks?

The answers to the questions above will reveal a great bit of insight that, if you respond honestly, will help you develop an effective goal-setting strategy. The answers will also reveal the changes you need to make in your own life—from the daily rituals you employ to the relationships you have established and continue to cultivate,

some of which need to be changed in order to grow. You can typically tell whether you need to make changes even before the specifics
are revealed because of the stress associated with the consequences
of your ongoing decisions. The clean slate exercise is a great way to
hone in on the specifics and reduce some of the stress in your life.

Service Before Self

During my service in the United States Air Force, I learned the
core values of this specific branch of the military—*Integrity First,
Service before Self, and Excellence in all we do.* These core values
are actually quite applicable to most anything worthwhile we do in
life. Most goals are tied in some manner to service—especially ones
that provide an increase in value and, ultimately, our net worth by
providing that service. So, if your goals have anything to do with
service, pay close attention to the value your service brings to people.
The more value you bring, the more attractive your offer. The more
attractive your offer, the more people you will reach. Serve enough
people with value and you will never lack for anything in your life.

An accurate assessment of where you are in terms of providing
a valuable service is essential. If you're like most people, you have
a pretty good *idea* of the type of service you would like to bring to
people. And like most, you're starting at zero. In other words, you're
not currently providing this service. Your clean slate is essentially
an idea—great start. So, where do you go from here?

Place service and value as your top priorities. Every strategic
consideration, every question, and every calculated move should
address the effect it has on your target audience or customer. How
does your service improve, alter, or affect the lives of your customers? What is the inherent value of your service? Is it attractive?
Can it be monetized? (Most everything can be monetized.) Is it
compelling enough to drive a secondary word-of-mouth referral?
Is it something that can be sustained? If so, implement. If not, spend

some time refining but don't get lost in the details. Better to start than to overanalyze.

Because You Asked

I often tell my team and my clients that they can have, be, do, or become anything they desire if they are willing to do *one* thing—ask. Think about it…if it's a sale you wish to close you must ASK for the close. If it's a date you wish to have with someone, you must ASK for the date. If it is knowledge you need—ASK. Consider, for example, that if you need a business loan, the bank is not going to arbitrarily knock on your door and offer you money. You must ask. Whatever you desire of this one life you have, you *must* ask.

The *manner* in which we ask questions is also important and has everything to do with how our questions are answered. For example, if you want to earn a certain amount of money, you must ask yourself, "How can I begin earning $_____?" This is what I call the *next-generation goal mind method* of asking. It is positive-based and framed in a manner that prepares us to receive an empowering answer to the questions we ask. Consider the alternative, pessimistic approach…

"Why am I always broke?"

How do you feel when you read the question above? Does it make you feel as if an empowering revelation is on its way to you? I didn't think so. There's something about this next-generation goal mind method of asking that is bigger than our ability to fully appreciate. The manner in which we approach the ASK is a clear difference-maker in how we receive answers. Our questions will *always* be answered, so we must be careful how we frame them, because we will always get what we ask for. If you ask how, your answer will show you. If you ask why, your answer will also show you. It is always better to frame our question in a manner that will provide insight as opposed to telling you what you already know. For example…

"How can I begin earning an extra $5,000 per month?" This question, once asked, elicits an *insightful* response that will lead you to people, ideas, and opportunities that will provide solutions designed to increase your income.

"Why am I always broke?" This question, once asked, will provide an answer to the reasons you are broke. Of course, you already *know* why. However, the answer could, in fact, provide some candid insight or clarity that may also be helpful in finding a way out of your insufficiency. It's just not the best approach to seek empowering answers.

Once you ask, your responsibility at that point is to expect an answer. That's right, you have every right to *expect* an answer. Keep in mind, however, that the answers you receive may not be *exactly* what you expect. But when the answers come—and they will come—you must *take action*. Your action completes the process of the next-generation goal mind method of asking. This powerful concept works *every* time.

Try it today: Look around you and identify people who are living the kind of life you want to live or earning the kind of money you want to earn. What are *they* doing that you're not? What special skills, methods, or abilities have they developed that you have not yet developed? What choices have they made that you haven't? What habits or rituals do they have? If you are not sure, seek them out and *ask*. Chances are they have a lot of the answers you seek because they have likely gone before you and asked some of the same questions themselves. Many of these people are more than willing to help you if you'll just…ask.

Consider Reinventing Yourself

I was talking to a young man recently about the value of a formal education. He is a sophomore at a central Florida college and is considering dropping out to pursue an Internet marketing career. He is an intellect with a solid understanding of marketing and social media. Our discussion led to learning methodologies and whether college was even relevant in this day and age. In the interest of full disclosure, it is fair to note that I am a former adjunct professor for a big named private college, so you can imagine my opinion when this young man explained why he wanted to drop out of school.

Wait...on second thought, perhaps you *cannot* imagine my opinion. You see, while I am a product of formal academia, I am *not* a staunch advocate that a formal education is the sole path to success and achievement. In fact, more and more millionaires without a college degree are emerging. A recent issue of *Forbes* reports that, out of the 400 richest people in America, 63 entrepreneurs don't have a college degree. What does this prove? Well, according to the young man I interviewed, aside from some rather interesting college courses (philosophy, business, psychology, etc.) he can learn most anything he wants from the Internet and do it faster and cheaper than traditional academia. I'd say he's onto something. And for the record, this young man already has over 7 million (yes, *seven million*) Instagram followers that he has monetized to well over six figures per year. How's that for an education?

How many people do you know that have a college degree who are unable to find a "college-level" entry position in the workplace? Some are doing well just to find a managerial position in a retail chain or outlet. Some are actually taking on second jobs just to make ends meet and pay down college debt. Make no mistake, I'm not suggesting anyone drop out of school to pursue their goals. What I *am* saying is that a formal education is not the *only* means to your desired objectives.

What about you? Where do you stand? Does your education enhance the advancement of your goals? Are you truly happy doing what you're doing? If so, great. If not, it may be time to consider an alternate approach. In fact, it may be time to reinvent yourself.

Reinvention calls upon you to listen to the subtle voice of reason—or, for some of you, the bullhorn that's screaming at you—to change course and move on to something different. The thought of reinvention can be a bit scary, but if you consider the alternative of "playing it safe," you have much to gain by following your instincts and the allure of doing something more meaningful with your life.

So, take a good look at where you are versus where you'd like to be. Is your current job preventing you from reaching your goals? Are you operating squarely in the lane of what brings you joy and meaning? If you know without a doubt that you are capable of so much more, then put some serious thought into the concept of reinvention.

Consider the possible scenario that your job or industry suddenly disappears. What would you do? You would have little choice but to reinvent yourself. Reinvention is nothing more than taking an alternate course of action for your life. For some of you, that can be a rather frightening thing to consider. You always have a choice, however. You can choose fear or liberation. It all depends on how determined (or desperate) you are. So, what would you do differently if you allowed yourself to make better use of your talents, skills, and interests to make a living? Think about how liberating that would be. Think about how much happier you could be.

I know a woman who had a secure job that produced a respectable wage. By most accounts, she was making about 20% more than the average wage for her geographic area. She called me one sunny afternoon and asked me to meet with her. When we met, she explained to me how miserable she was in her job. Despite the income and security, she was not operating in her lane of passion. She had recently taken up an interest in a totally different area than she had ever experienced and was happiest pursuing that new interest. Despite the risk to her immediate income and comfort level, she met with me to declare her intent to pursue her new interest…and to seek my perspective on whether she was making the right decision to reinvent herself. I congratulated her on her ability to listen to the higher calling, respond to that call, and demonstrate her intent by telling someone—me. Of course, I reminded her that the decision was her own and not one I would dissuade nor encourage. But her story reminds us all that, in order to find true happiness, such a bold decision is sometimes in order.

You are capable of doing many different things. You have a wide variety of skills, abilities, knowledge, talents, education, and experience. There are many jobs and tasks you could do, or learn to do, extremely well. Never allow yourself to get trapped in a particular job or lifestyle, especially if you are not happy with the way things are going for yourself. Some of the happiest people I know are doing what they love. Shouldn't you be doing the same?

History 101

There's a lot to be gained from taking a look at the past in terms of lessons learned and the value those lessons have for the promise of your future. However, you should avoid allowing history to negatively influence your capabilities. Doing so *could* cause you to short-change yourself in terms of the value you have to give and the joy you have yet to receive. Just because history shows how many times you fell short of a goal or objective should *never* serve as an indication that you cannot overcome past experiences and discover a breakthrough that finally works. Ignoring the *lessons* of the past is rarely a good idea, while ignoring the *effects* of the past may be a worthwhile consideration, especially if those effects hold you back.

You can never erase the past, but you <u>can</u> overcome it.

The value of history provides you with insight, perspective, and self-awareness. These three elements alone put you in a power position to succeed far more than most any other aspect of goal-setting.

The power is in the knowing, which goes hand-in-hand with your intent to bring about the realization of your goal. Insight, perspective, and awareness are absolute essentials. Without these elements, your goal attainment process lacks the engine it requires to get you from where you are to where you're going.

Accelerate Your Way to Achievement

You have an incredible capacity to master most anything you truly desire to accomplish. Of course, you already know this. You also most likely already know how setting goals for your life and making detailed plans to achieve them will save years of hard work in reaching your objectives. What you may *not* know is how to accelerate the process.

We all know that goal-setting is arguably one of the most important steps to success. But let's be honest: sometimes traditional methods are not the most efficient. The lives we lead today are characterized by bits, bytes, slices, samples, and fragments of input and information, all competing for our time and attention. We have become quite adept at giving each competing element enough time and attention to draw a snap conclusion on whether it is worth a second look or deeper investment of our precious time. We spend so much of that time managing the things coming at us from every conceivable angle that looking into the future to determine our goals becomes an afterthought, *if* it even places that high on our list of priorities. So, here's how to accelerate your way to achievement by adding a twist to the traditional goal-setting concept and into what I call *goal-mapping*.

Goal-Mapping

Take a moment to imagine yourself where you will be one year from today. Are you there? Good. Now, here's where your absolute honesty comes into play. How do you see your life as you take stock of it one year from today? Is it much different from what you currently see when you look at your life today?

This simple exercise can be rather sobering, as a majority of people I have taken through this visualization process don't see much of a difference in one year from the current state of their life. Why? Because they haven't given themselves permission to remove the limitations of their imagination.

Removing the self-imposed limitations can be a tricky process for some people. In working with people from across the spectrum, I have found that there are two camps when it comes to removing self-imposed limitations. The first group of people merely need a *reminder* that they have the capacity to create a vision of the kind of life they want. Once reminded, these people get to work on creating their one-year life vision. The other group of people require a bit more coaching. Theirs is typically a process that requires them to identify the obstacles that are preventing them from using the full capacity of their imagination. Until the limits of your imagination are set aside, you will not be in a position to accelerate your goal achievement process.

Things Are Not Always What They Seem

Indulge me for just a bit as I demonstrate how we so often buy into the convincing nature of our imagination. I tell a short story at some of my presentations to help people become aware of the limits they unwittingly place on their imagination. I begin the story by telling the audience to set their imaginations free, to imagine *anything* they like inside the premise of the story. With this permission as a basis and agreement by the audience, I begin to tell them the story.

"Imagine…you're boarding an airliner to a dream vacation destination. You are greeted by the friendly flight attendant and make your way down the aisle to your seat. Once you find your seat and settle in, you fasten your seat belt. Shortly thereafter, you hear the captain's voice come across the cabin loudspeakers. 'Ladies and gentlemen, this is the captain. Welcome aboard ABC Airlines. Our destination today is _____. We'll be cruising at an altitude of thirty-thousand feet. The weather is clear and should make for a very comfortable and enjoyable flight. If there's anything we can do for you, please don't hesitate to ask. Meantime, sit back, relax, and enjoy the flight. Once again, welcome aboard.'"

Once I finish telling the audience the story, I ask how many of them could "see" themselves as they entered the aircraft. Most every hand goes up. Then I ask them if they could "see" themselves finding their seat. Again, most every hand goes up. Then I pause slightly and ask, "For all of you who saw yourself boarding the aircraft and finding your seat, how many of you found a seat in *coach class*?" Most every hand goes up as the audience quickly discovers the limits they have placed on their imaginations.

Inside the power of your imagination, you don't have to sit in coach class. You are free to sit anywhere you desire. You could realistically choose to sit in the cockpit if you like. Why then do we place limits on our imagination? Because our imagination is programmed based on what we have been exposed to in life. As understandable as that fact may be, it is time to remove the limitations of your imagination.

Now, with the limits of your imagination in check, reimagine your future self, one year from today. Describe your life in detail. Revisit the first section of this chapter for a reminder on the importance of including the details into your one-year vision (sight, sound, touch, taste). Only now, be even *more* specific. Imagine starting your day waking up in a place you are meant to be, a place you *desire* to be...a place you have worked hard to be. As you lie in your brand-new bed and look around at your new surroundings, think back upon the past year and admire what you have accomplished.

Allow your future self to draw the contrasts between where you are and where you were just one year earlier. What changed? What was it that brought you here? What *one* change did you make, among all others, that made the most difference in terms of what it took to *accelerate* your progress?

The vision of your one-year self should be a euphoric experience. In other words, it should stir your emotions. If it does not, go back and work on that imagination a bit more. Remember, inside your imagination there are no limits!

When you know where you are, you have a starting point. Then, when you look backward from your future self in one year (or any timeline you choose), you have an end point. I know I don't have to explain the obvious, but when you have a starting point *and* an ending point, you have a map. When you have a map, you have a plan. If you can follow a plan (map), then you can easily get to your desired destination. You can effectively reach your goals. Many people have used this concept to 10-X their goal achievement process. I have received more feedback on the powerful simplicity of this concept than most any other method of achievement strategies I have employed.

> *Successful people employ successful strategies to achieve extraordinarily successful results.*

The goal-mapping process is influenced by how we think. We generally fall into one of two broad thinking tendency styles that are governed by right-brain/left brain science. The left brain is largely responsible for the logic and facts that we process. The right brain processes emotions, pictures, and sounds.

Scientists believe people are either predominantly right-brained or predominantly left-brained, just as people are predominantly right-handed or left-handed (by the way, right- or left-handed tendencies have not been scientifically correlated with right- or left-brained predominance). Given that, it's important to note that, as we apply ourselves to the goal-setting (and goal-getting) process, we should be mindful to use both sides of our brain. Doing so provides an undeniably convincing message to our subconscious minds using the leverage that both sides of the brain collectively provide.

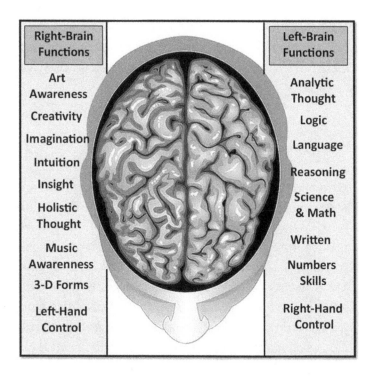

So, how do you know whether you are predominantly right-brained or left-brained? To answer this question, take a look at the graphic above. Read the elements describing each side to determine which of the descriptions best describe your tendencies. As you take a broader look at the graphic, consider whether you are intrigued at all with the picture in the middle of the graphic. If so, then you are definitely right-brain predominant (as I am).

In Summary

If you had a map that you knew led to a buried treasure worth $1 million, how would your life change? How would your priorities change? Would you be as easily distracted by the pettiness of life (TV, social media, partying, personalities…)? Would you have the courage to say *no* to the people and distractions that keep you from making your way to the treasure? Absolutely not, because *none* of these elements contribute to you reaching your goal. Successful people know where they are going in life. They have a vision that drives them every…single…day. Shouldn't *you* at least consider doing the same?

Some Final Thoughts

> ➢ **Begin with a clean slate.** Remember to conduct an initial assessment of where you are currently. It is absolutely essential you be honest with yourself during this process. This is not a time for pride to get in the way. Everything you hope to gain is based upon your honest assessment of where you are in terms of what and who you know. This will reveal what and who you *don't* know, which provides you with a great starting point (a clean slate) to begin your journey. This clean slate approach provides you with the critical elements of insight and awareness, which is absolutely essential to the goal-achievement process.

> ➢ **Ask the right questions in the right way.** The manner in which we ask questions is important and has everything to do with how our questions are answered. Your ability to ask the right questions opens a treasure trove of information, connections, and opportunities that will astound you. Feel free to test the next-generation goal mind method of asking and see the amazing changes that take place in your life just

by asking. Start with something small, like a good night's sleep. Yes, if you can remember to ASK for a good night of sleep, you will in fact sleep better. If it will work for something as simple as a good night of sleep, imagine what it will do for whatever else you can think of to ask.

➢ **Reinvent yourself if you must.** The term reinvention can be so intimidating, especially when it directly affects the foundational core of who you are (or what you have become familiar with). If what you are currently doing is not working for you…if your career or your initiatives are not supporting the advancement of your desired goals, you may want to consider reinventing yourself. Reinvention is a decision you make to transform yourself from where you are to where you want to be. Reinvention requires you to think differently in order to become something different—something more in line with your passion and purpose.

➢ **Accelerate your results.** Remove the self-imposed limitations of your imagination and project yourself to a point in time where you can look back and see with clarity the steps you need to take to achieve your goals. Once you have a map, you can easily get from where you are to where you want to be. But it's up to you to create the map.

Thought-provoking questions…

1. Your life is a clean slate. If *anything* were possible and there were *no* risks of failure, what would you immediately set out to do?

2. Who do you know that has achieved the kind of success you hope to achieve? Do you have access to them or someone

close to them who can arrange a meeting? Be sure to bring value and respect their time.

3. What would you do if your job or industry were suddenly obsolete? What would happen if the safety net suddenly disappeared? Can you think of ways to provide more value inside the line of work you currently do?

4. Are you asking the right questions to get to the right information you seek? Are you expecting answers, or have you forgotten to watch for them? Are you prepared to take action when the answers reveal themselves?

Chapter Four

Opportunity Knocks

**"I am not what happens to me,
I am what I choose to become."**
~ Carl Gustav Jung

Desperation can be a life-changing experience. As a young man in my twenties, I had no money and no sense on how to use what little income I had. Despite the fact that I had a steady job in the Air Force, it didn't pay well. I was an Airman, which is to say, I was in the lowest echelon of pay grades. A study once conducted by the US Census Bureau placed an Airman's income *below* the national poverty line. We actually qualified for food stamps and government assistance programs...and I was *in* the government! Things were so bad financially that I had resorted to purchasing diapers and baby formula for my newborn daughter using what was left on a nearly maxed-out credit card. As I said, I wasn't very good with money and mishandled what little we had with poor financial decision-making skills.

I hit an all-time low in the checkout line of a local grocery store one day when my credit card was denied—bread, milk, and baby formula waiting to be paid for on the conveyor belt in front of me. I walked away from the checkout line empty-handed, dejected, and embarrassed as I made my way to my over-used, worn-out car and turned the key. Nothing. The battery was dead. They say timing is everything. *This* timing was literally overwhelming.

There I sat—the weight of the world upon my shoulders and an expectant wife and newborn daughter waiting for me to arrive home with a few bare essentials from the grocery store—unable to move or take care of my most basic obligations. I placed my face into my hands and started to cry. It was the worst feeling of helplessness I had ever known.

As I sat in my broken car with a broken spirit, it suddenly occurred to me that if anything was *ever* going to change, I knew *I* would have to be the one to change first. It was right then and there that I resolved *never* to be in such a position again. I guess you could describe my epiphany as a collision of all my emotions—fear, anger, intolerance, and stress—all coming together at once. Whatever it was, something changed within me, and I could sense it. I was suddenly more determined than ever to overcome my circumstances and find a way not only to survive but to *thrive*.

After I collected myself, I got out of the car and opened the hood, determined to figure out my mechanical issue. A nice gentleman approached and kindly offered to help me by jump-starting my battery. Our small talk led the discussion to my desperate financial situation, which led to him offering me a part-time job at his furniture store. I accepted, even though I knew I'd have to clear it first with my primary employer. The Air Force agreed, and I began working while reconstructing my life, my mindset, and my financial situation.

To this day, I still remember the moment I had made the decision to take responsibility for my life. It was as if I had discovered an entirely new perspective of myself. I would learn later, in retrospect, that it was a turning point—a defining moment—that brought about a transition in me from adolescence to adulthood...from acceptance to determination.

*"A man is nothing else than what
he makes of himself."*
~ Jean-Paul Sartre

Sadly, there are people who never make the transition from acceptance to determination. These people are the same ones who insist on blaming everything and *everyone* for their circumstances. Thankfully, there are many others who are of a far different mindset. I talk with people from all over the world in all walks of life in every conceivable situation and circumstance. I can tell you there is great clarity offered by the perspective of an open mind. For me, it took a significant emotional event to find the resolve to change my life by opening my own mind to reveal the things I was doing wrong in order to begin to learn what to do right.

I find it refreshing to speak to people who are ready and willing to step out of their own way long enough to listen to insight, wisdom, and a few simple steps to completely turn their lives around. Most people are simply trapped in a life they have allowed their mind to create. Once they discover they have the *power* to break free from that life to one they can actually direct…it is simply a *magical* thing to observe. It is as if I am witnessing an actual transformation taking place before me in real time, all because of a willingness to seize an opportunity to improve.

If *you* are ready to seize the opportunity, to take control of your life, and to witness your *own* transition, then you've found yourself at the right place, on the right page, and in the right frame of mind. Opportunity is all about timing and a willingness to seize the moment. So, fasten your seat belt, set your biases aside, and open your mind to the concepts that are outlined on the remaining pages of this book.

Don't Be Your Own Worst Enemy

Of all we have to fend off in this world, the *last* thing we should ever be concerned about is ourselves. Yet, all too often *we* become the primary obstacle leading to our own inadequacies. There are several reasons for this. Chief among them is our inability (or unwillingness) to rationalize the implementation of a sound strategy and the inconsistency of effective follow-through.

Even the *best* plans, driven by the *best* goals, can fall prey to apathy and the allure of a convenient and busy lifestyle. We are lured away far too easily from a directed path by the sensory overload of all that is conveniently available to us—most all of which was initially intended to enrich the quality of our lives. Yet, these very same conveniences are largely responsible for disrupting the path of the goals we desire in our attempt to create a better life. Television, cell phones, and computers are among the primary distractors we face on a daily basis. Americans watch more television than any other demographic on earth. We are electronically "overconnected" by the overreliance of our cell phones. Don't think so? Ever watched our younger generation having a conversation with each other without uttering an audible word, heads down, buried in the mesmerizing allure of their digital devices? Hello? They're most likely texting each other and saying things most parents would find surprising, to say the least. But I digress.

Goal achievement requires *action*. It has also become entirely too easy for us to rationalize a *delay* in action because of the higher priorities of a busy life that *we* are largely responsible for creating to begin with. If your life has become so busy that you have little or no time to or for yourself, you will have difficulty finding the time required to create any real momentum your goals require. Instead, you will develop only frustration, which will eventually lead to other, more destructive, negative emotions (anger, resentment, fear, etc.). The good news is that this can be easily overcome with the right mindset adjustments.

The right mindset is absolutely essential to effective goal achievement. The *right mindset* is simply defined as a willingness to see things differently. So how do we do that?

Fear

Most of what we fear is based on the unknown. Simply stated, we fear what we cannot see or understand. The lack of a crystal-clear vision leads to distortion and uncertainty. These conditions leave our dreams subject to fear because we neglect to remove uncertainty by clearly defining our objectives. As a result, we rob ourselves of an ability to *see* and therefore begin a destructive process of self-sabotage through the effects of fear. Doubt sets in as we focus on everything standing in our way of achievement. We take our eyes off the goal and instead focus on the obstacles. We inevitably relent by redefining our goals by accepting less than we deserve or giving up on them altogether.

There are two schools of thought concerning fear when it comes to achieving our goals. Both are driven by the philosophy of emotion, as mentioned earlier: a desire to *gain* something and a desire to *protect* something.

Fear can play havoc on our ability to reach our goals if it is driven by a desire to gain something. We are rarely successful if our goals are supported by a premise of fear that we are somehow unable to do the things necessary to achieve them. If, on the other hand, our fear of loss or injury is strong enough to compel us into action, there won't be much that can withstand our desire to do whatever it takes to reach a goal or objective that supports our self-preservation. It is not the preferred method of goal-setting, but it has been known to work quite well at times.

"The only thing we have to fear is fear itself."
~ Franklin D. Roosevelt

The absolute *best* way to achieve any goal or objective is, as mentioned earlier, with a clearly-defined plan of action firmly rooted by a well-defined vision of our objectives. In other words, we must know what it is we want—in essence, where we are going (our destination)—and to make sure it is clearly defined. When you think of your goal, can you literally *see* it in your mind? What color is it? How does it make you feel? What other senses are involved? Is it something you can smell, touch, taste, or hear? If so, use your senses to draw clarity into crystal clear focus. You will be amazed at the difference it makes in your ability to progress toward your goals.

Our goals drive our strategy, which drives our action plan. Don't ever allow fear to rob you of achievement. The most powerful weapon you have is your power of choice. Make a choice to define your objectives with clarity. Only then can you draft an effective strategy to go after your goals.

Circumstance

Our lives reflect the sum total of the choices and decisions we have made to this very point. Those choices and decisions form the basis of what we consider to be our circumstances. Circumstance is less significant than we believe it to be when it comes to goal achievement. In fact, circumstance has been overcome so many times it has proven to be a condition that serves as more of an illusion than an obstacle. Of course, that is not to say that some circumstances are indeed not genuine obstacles that must be effectively overcome in order to pursue our objectives. The significance of circumstance rests in your resolve to eliminate or overcome them in order to live beyond them.

Read that again and allow it to sink in. Do not allow circumstance to rob you of the ability to overcome and achieve your goals.

Far too many people live life according to their circumstances. Ask them how they're doing, and they respond, "I'm well…under the circumstances." My response is to simply get out from under the circumstances. To remain shackled by circumstance is a personal choice. These people *choose* to employ a mindset that allows circumstance to control them. They employ an "if only, then" mentality. They say things like, "*If only* I could win the lottery, *then* I'd be happy," or "*If only* I had purchased real estate five years ago, *then* I'd be wealthy." As the great Jim Rohn used to say, "For things to change, *you* have to change yourself."

If you are looking for ordinary, then perhaps you don't mind being *under the circumstances*. But if you're looking for extraordinary, then you most certainly would agree that you need to get *beyond* the circumstances that are standing in your way of achieving your goals.

You can rest assured that *no* negative circumstance has the power to prevent you from moving your life forward. You can easily move forward and mitigate negative circumstance simply by creating meaning in your life. How? Through love, through work, and through relentless tenacity.

- ➢ Love – Cultivate and nurture loving relationships that make living worthwhile.

- ➢ Work – Create a dream that *inspires* you more than your negative circumstances drain you.

- ➢ Tenacity – Take pride in how you react to circumstance through a positive outlook. And never, ever quit!

Determine your Desire

Is your goal compelling enough for you to say *no* to distractions? Does it have the power to drive you and motivate you to be different from most everyone else? Is it strong enough for you to say no to friends and family when they invite you to join them at an event, taking time that could otherwise be spent pursuing your goal? If it is not, then you either need to redefine your goal or you need a new one. Don't get me wrong, friends—okay, scratch that—*family* is important. But even *they* must understand if you are pursuing a goal and choose to say *no* on occasion. If your family is not supportive, then you will find yourself at a crossroads where you must make yet another critical decision to delay or abandon your goals. No one is judging here, but the fact remains that a certain amount of dedication is required of any goal. Some of those decisions call for tough choices. The degree and direction your desires and commitments take you is *always* yours to determine.

Goal achievement requires an unwavering, burning desire, action, and effective follow-through. Desire is created by an attraction to something we believe will enhance the quality of our lives. If that desire is compelling enough, we will go to great lengths to achieve the goal it is attached to.

A strong desire has "special powers," or so it seems. Think about the last time you truly desired something (or someone). Chances are, there was little to nothing that had a chance of standing in your way of the achievement of your desire. If you can remember and relate to this unrelenting feeling of power, then that is *exactly* the level of commitment you need to achieve most any goal you set for yourself.

Desire is the catalyst that will help you get past inevitable distractions and set you on your way to achievement, but desire is only the beginning—admittedly a very *powerful* beginning—but a beginning nonetheless. So, you have a desire…a *burning* desire to achieve your goal. Now what?

*To succeed, your desire to change must be
greater than your desire to stay the same.*

Lights, Camera…ACTION!

Something magical happens when we turn on the lights. Quite simply, we can see! In order to go beyond desire in the goal attainment process, we must be able to clearly identify that which we cannot currently see. The first step to gain clarity in formulating our goal is to identify *why* we want to attain it. This is one of the most important aspects in the goal process, so put some thought here. Don't just say, "I want to find love," or "I want to get wealthier." Discover *why* you want to find love. *Why* do you want to be wealthy? Is your motivation driven by desire, fear, or anger? It's okay to tap into those emotions until you can transition to greater clarity. Without a compelling reason *why,* we remain disconnected, and our efforts are subject to the risk of failure, stagnation, and frustration.

Perspective is everything. Who among us has taken a picture and not been absolutely *compelled* to see it right away? Why do we do that? Well, some of us want to make sure we actually look good. One way we do that is by looking at ourselves from the alternate perspective of a camera lens—a photograph. For the best perspective of our self, we must examine things from a selfless point of view.

Once we have identified our why, and we have a clearer perspective of our self, we are ready for the third step—*Action!* This third step, quite simply, is *doing it*. Sounds simple enough. But, unfortunately, this is where most people fall short. In order for any goal to materialize, *you must act* on it. It is a universal law of nature. Without action, nothing happens. So, make something happen!

CAUTION! An attack on the integrity of your desire will inevitably occur from time to time, so keep up your guard. Of all the sources that are likely to test your desire, those posing the most danger come from within. That's right, *we* are our own worst enemy. Here are some warning signs you should be aware of that have the potential to prevent you from ever achieving your goals. Defeat them and you will be well on your way to achievement.

Excuses, Rationalization, and Justifications

Ever wonder how some people seem to be able to get so much done during the same 24-hour period the rest of us have? While some people make excuses, achievers make *progress*. They refuse to blame circumstance or other people for an inadequacy or unwillingness to act. They accept *full* responsibility for their actions (or inactions). Some people believe excuses remove blame from themselves. Nothing could be further from the truth. Excuses are fairly easily recognized and are an ill-advised approach to take for anyone serious about achieving goals.

Excuses lead us down a path of underachievement, mediocrity, and eventual obscurity. You don't want that, or you wouldn't be reading this book. So, stop justifying, rationalizing, and making excuses. Stop looking for reasons why you *cannot* take action and begin, *right now*, to take a stand against any tendency to make excuses. See excuses for what they are—obstacles you can easily overcome to begin achieving your goals.

If some of your obstacles are *not* easy to overcome, then accept it, don't rationalize it. Rationalization always displaces the focus away from what you *are* doing to what you *should* be doing. People who rationalize cast themselves as a victim. Victims typically identify themselves based on attributes of powerlessness, dependency, entitlement, apathy, worry, fear, and self-doubt. A victim lives at the effect of what happens around them, oftentimes adopting circumstance as an excuse *not* to act or, at best, to embrace delay. So, stand tall and eliminate the tendency to rely on excuses. Your ability to refrain from making excuses will take you to a place where clarity exists. Your clarity will reveal ways you can overcome obstacles and begin realizing your dreams.

Wisdom is reserved for those courageous enough to step beyond excuses.

Accept Responsibility

The *only* person accountable for your actions *and reactions* is you. Personal responsibility is a willingness to accept the standards we set for ourselves, without compromise, based principally on the manner in which we perceive those standards. In other words, it is our "response-ability," or our ability to respond appropriately to the varying and ever-changing challenges of life that determines the conditions of our circumstances, and not the other way around.

Want a better life? Then consider the manner in which you respond to life. The quality and tempo of our lives is largely determined by the manner in which we respond to circumstances. "Now hold on just a second," you may declare. "Things happen to me all the time that I have no control over." That can certainly be true, and, while you may not be *in control* of everything that happens *around* you, your choice to see it as happening *to* you is a response choice you freely make. Remember, you are responsible for how you think, act, and feel in response to everything, period.

Far too many people view responsibility as a matter of obligation or of having duties of some kind. Few other virtues have as significant an effect on your life as taking responsibility. Accepting personal responsibility comes with empowering qualities that put you in the driver's seat of your life. Your admission and acceptance of responsibility immediately reveals just how much power and influence you truly have. Suddenly, any goal you wish to achieve is within your grasp to control and obtain.

Personal responsibility is part of the foundation of personal development. By acknowledging your role in the goal achievement process, you open the door of opportunity through the self-improvement process.

Okay, so we must take responsibility. Easy, right? Not so fast. While the *concept* may be relatively easy to understand, the *application* of accepting responsibility can be met with certain roadblocks. One of the roadblocks is a tendency to blame others for our own oversight, shortcomings, or outright mistake or misinterpretation. We must first resist any temptation of blaming others.

The Buck Stops Here

The 33rd President of the United States, Harry Truman, had a sign on his desk that read, "The Buck Stops Here." It was a mantra he adopted, determined to accept full responsibility for the role he had as America's leader. It also served notice to all that he had no intention of blaming others for anything he could control or otherwise influence. Each and every one of us can learn a thing or two from the spirit of this attitude.

Blaming others serves only to hold the blamer hostage. It serves no other purpose. Blaming others displaces the solution focus, complicates progress, and steals away your power. From now on, refuse to blame anyone for anything—past, present, or future. If you make a mistake or miscalculation, take ownership and get busy rectifying it.

Control Your Emotions

Emotional intelligence is defined as having an ability to self-manage our own emotions *and* the emotions of others. Self-management describes our ability to use the awareness of our emotions to actively choose what we say and do, regardless of the circumstances. If you have ever found yourself reacting to your emotions before you have had enough time to process the actual information—as I have done at times—you know all too well that, most times, our initial reactions are incorrect and generally not in our best interest.

There are subtle things you can do each and every day to influence what is happening just beneath the surface of your interactions with the people and the world around you (hence my comment on managing the emotions of others). These subtleties can lead to a higher level of self-awareness that allow you to get out of your own way as you begin to see things as they are, instead of how you've pre-programmed them to be.

> **Breathe** – That's right, breathe. The simple act of taking a breath can often be the difference-maker in terms of allowing us enough time to mentally process a situation unfolding before us.

> **Listen** – Active listening is a skill we develop through the tenets of practice and compassion. Active listening places us in line with the accuracy of what is being said, how it is being delivered, and the context in which it is conveyed.

> **Empathize** – Put yourself in the position of others. Doing so will provide one of the greatest gifts we can use to control our emotions—empathy through perspective. We never truly know the plight of others until we take the time to consider that there may be more there than meets the eye.

> **Self-Regulate** – People who self-regulate typically do not allow their emotions to get the best of them (think anger or jealousy). They don't make impulsive or careless decisions. They think before they act.

When you understand your own emotions, you begin to respond to them differently. You will begin seeing situations differently, giving you the time to react differently to the changes occurring around you at any given moment. Everything around you—your physical surroundings, nature, people—comes alive with your renewed sense of awareness. And that awareness will change you and show you things you never would have seen without it.

You Get to Choose

One of the greatest powers we have as humans is the power of choice. Unless we're incarcerated, we have great latitude on our ability to choose. The content and quality of our lives to this very moment is largely determined by the sum total of all the choices and decisions we have made along the way. If there is anything in your life you are unhappy about, *you* are responsible for making the choices required to change the direction. The best part about that statement is that *you get to choose*. That's where choice aligns itself beautifully with setting goals. As I clearly lay out in my book, *Fear Is a Thief*…

Our life experiences are largely determined by the way we react to everything that happens to us or around us, in addition to the choices we make along the way. It means never blaming others for the way we feel, the fears we experience, and the life we lead. By the same token, we should never blame ourselves, because doing so is destructive and counterproductive to the process of overcoming fear and ultimately diminishes our ability to enjoy the nuances of life. It also breeds resentment, turmoil, and frustration.

Here is a controversial statement (unless you understand the power of choice in its full context)…

You are earning today exactly what you have decided to earn.

If you are unhappy with your level of income, make a decision to change it. Set a goal, make a plan, and take action on the things you need to do to bring your goals to reality. Look for opportunities, get a part-time job to earn additional income, take a class to learn a new skill to increase your abilities or capacity to serve others, or learn to communicate better so you can express yourself more clearly to those who will hire or promote you. Your refusal to consider any or all of these options could be the very reason you are...unhappily earning what you are earning.

The quality of your choices is absolutely critical to the successful outcome of your goals. In fact, your choice of a mate or partner and your choice of friends will have as much or *more* to do with your success and happiness than any other decisions you will make. Why do we seem to learn that after we have allowed our emotions to overcome our logic?

You are in charge of research and development, personal training, and learning. It is up to you, and you alone, to determine the talents, skills, abilities, and core competencies you will need to earn the kind of money you want to earn and live the kind of life you want to live in the months and years ahead. It is *your* responsibility to make the investment and take the time to learn and develop these skills and to find a balance between emotion and logic. No one is going to do it for you.

The unavoidable truth is that no one really cares as much as you do, nor should they. But as you begin realizing your goals, people will naturally be drawn to you, wondering how *you* can do it while they cannot. The irony is, there will be other people of great influence who will also be drawn to you for entirely different reasons. This is where the opening of opportunity exists. Choose wisely.

Think Strategically

I often used to wonder what made the difference between those who are successful and those who are not. By "successful" I mean those who seem to be able to achieve most anything they set their mind to in order to bring about a quantifiable outcome—results. As I took a deeper look at things, I began to understand that outcomes are driven by *forces*, not all of which are readily apparent. So, I began looking at things from the inside-out, which was more of an intuitive move on my part than anything else. Turns out, there was more to my instincts than I first realized.

Results, I learned, are typically materialized by the law of cause and effect. The *effect*, in this case, is tied directly to the achievement of success in whatever form we can imagine or readily define. The *cause* is the culmination of everything we must *do* in order to achieve the effect.

I learned that the one compelling reason we do anything is tied directly to *why* we do it. The why is driven by emotions and is closely connected to the level of effort we're willing to put forth to attain pleasure or avoid pain.

Whether we achieve success to any great degree depends largely upon three basic principles I call *The Triple-S Theory*: our *Story*, our *Strategy*, and our *State*. Each deserves some elaboration, so I've decided to focus on them separately as the concepts in this book naturally call for them. We have already elaborated on our *Story* in Chapter Two. Now, let's take a look at how an effective strategy can influence the outcome of your goals.

I've written extensively on the importance of having a plan for success. Our plan is driven by the *Strategy* we employ to achieve our objectives. Without a strategy to support our vision, dream, goal, destination, or objective, there is no point in taking any action whatsoever, else we find ourselves running off in random directions essentially achieving little more than frustration.

Unfortunately, most people stop just after the *vision* part and, all too often, fail to enact any kind of strategy to put their vision on a map and get started with the process of achievement and the pursuit of success. Without a strategy, all that essentially exists is a dream or a vision, which is indeed a vital part of the process. But a dream or vision by itself does little more than create a fleeting fantasy that reinforces the notion that dreams can never really be achieved. Don't buy in to that notion for one second!

As an air traffic controller, I would meticulously examine the flight plan of each and every aircraft under my control. The flight plan defines the pilot's intended course of action—the strategy—designed to reach an objective, in this case, the intended destination. Success in aviation is defined as the safe and uneventful journey of an aircraft from takeoff to touchdown. In life, success is defined by our progressive journey to an ultimate achievement of some kind. We set a course by clearly defining our destination and by following a strategy to reach that objective.

The strength and reliability of our strategy rests upon our convictions. (There's that "why" again.) It goes without saying that if we are driven to achieve something—and if we want it bad enough—we'll find the right strategy. There is no better illustration of this than the dichotomy of the two opposing groups (those who are successful and those who are not).

The success of our strategy rests upon our daily rituals or behaviors, both of which are influenced by a mindset. If our rituals don't support our strategy, we will never make it to our objective. Our rituals include all of the obligations, distractions, and habits/routines we use to define the construct of our lives.

My curiosity to discover the differences between the two groups led to my own transformation as I began to make changes in my own rituals that better supported my goals. The differences were subtle at first but significant, nonetheless. The significance eventually turned into what I call "terminal velocity." The term relates to how small changes in behavior or strategy eventually reach a transition point of profound momentum, the likes of which produce amazing results! Isn't it time you thought more about *your* strategy?

Determine Your Angle of Influence

If you are like most people, you are heavily influenced by the things going on around you at any given moment. The fact that you are reading this book, however, can be an indicator that you are *not* like most people and you either have a desire or already know how to handle external influences. The fact remains, we *get to* decide how we are influenced and to what extent. Just knowing that fact empowers us far more than you may realize.

Most of us lean one way or another when it comes to the manner in which we allow influence to drive us. We are either "generally" *external* or "generally" *internal* to some varying degree. Obviously, each of us are slightly different in terms of how much we are pre-programmed for influence. The more external we are the more vulnerable we are to *outside* influences. The more internal we are the less vulnerable we are to outside influences.

A person who is internally driven is generally one who feels a greater sense of control. They self-identify with strength, confidence, and power. This personality-type is characteristically optimistic, positive, and driven. On the other hand, the person who is externally driven is one who often feels "controlled" by external factors—their boss, their bills, their marriage, their childhood, or their circumstances. They often feel more out of control than in control. When they are happy, nothing can stop them. When they are not, *nothing* can motivate them.

The starting point of goal-setting calls for a realization that you have unlimited potential to be, have, or do anything you want in life—if you simply want it badly enough and are willing to work long enough, hard enough, and smart enough to achieve it.

The second part of goal-setting is for you to accept complete responsibility for your life and for everything that happens to you, with no blaming and no excuses.

Some Final Thoughts

➤ **Get out of your own way.** Remove the limits of your imagination and know that you can have, be, or do anything in this life that you desire…as long as you truly desire it. Stop making excuses and start making your way toward your dreams, goals, and aspirations. Set that goal!

➤ **Determine your desire.** How much do you want to change your situation? Enough to say no to a few people for a while until your life begins to change? If not, you may not be ready to pursue your goal. In order to achieve most *worthy* goals, you must cultivate a burning desire. A burning desire is one that will help you get past inevitable obstacles and temptations. A burning desire also changes your mindset from ordinary to extraordinary and empowers you to succeed.

➤ **Accept responsibility.** Be mindful of your response to life's every input. The manner in which you react will determine your experiences in life. This powerful concept shows us that we can shape our own destiny just by the way we *respond* to everything from our conditions to our influences.

➤ **Think strategically.** Your strategy to reach your goal is an absolutely critical aspect of the entire achievement process. You must have a plan, you must develop a strategy to nurture it, and you must develop rituals that are in line with the things you wish to achieve. Your faithful consistency will pay off handsomely as you begin to witness the changes taking place in your life. Do not lose faith at this critical juncture, as it will only result in frustration and an acceptance of mediocrity.

➤ **Realign your influence**. If you recognize a need to shift your center of influence from an external perspective to an internal one, then practice the principles of avoiding the temptations that distract you from your goals. Learn the concept of temporary restraint for long-term gain. Your discipline will richly reward you in the end.

Thought-provoking questions...

1. Take a few moments to reflect upon your goals. What is preventing you from achieving them? In what ways are you responsible for your current situation?

2. Think about the relationships you have that are incongruent with the desired direction of your life. What changes can you make that will realign the path and motivate you to lean forward toward achievement? Who do you need to forgive in order to free *yourself* of the burden *you* carry?

3. How can you change your decision-making in order to better align yourself with your goals?

4. What can you do to begin taking responsibility for your actions and reactions to everything happening around you?

5. What small steps can you take to change the rituals you have that will free up the time you need to focus on your efforts toward the achievement of your goals?

Chapter Five

The Future

The future belongs to those who have the courage to create it. Courage is an interesting word. The essence of courage implies we must face something in order to overcome it. Ask anyone who has achieved any level of success and they will tell you they had the *courage* to follow their convictions and were not afraid to be different.

Success, by most measures, is typically identified as something we *attract* into our lives by following our convictions. A conviction is a firmly held belief or opinion that drives or motivates us. It is the incentive we use to keep moving forward as we pursue our goals. Our convictions provide a foundation of courage, allowing us to prevail against obstacles and difficulties that will inevitably appear in our life from time to time. The strength of our convictions is directly proportional to the future of our success.

When you follow your convictions, people notice. As people notice, your path becomes better defined and begins to take shape.

It begins to evidence itself outwardly. As the growth process takes place, the seeds of your vision take hold and become rooted in those very convictions. The decision to take the first step demonstrates your courage and is driven by the belief you have in yourself, your ideas, and your motivations. The result is a personal transformation manifested by the courage to follow through and pursue your dreams, goals, and visions...no matter what.

Effective goal-setting requires you to rely upon the use of your imagination. But it is more than that. As important as it is to use your imagination, it is equally important to engage your convictions. In other words, you must *believe* you can achieve the very things you imagine. To develop, foster, and ground your convictions, consider employing the practices and philosophies in this book. These fundamentals will help you take the necessary steps to frame your belief in the goals you set and the achievements you will reach in what the future holds for you.

While appearing as a guest speaker at a music and tech expo, modern-day visionary and SpaceX founder Elon Musk spoke candidly about his ambitions to establish a colony on Mars. "The Moon and Mars are often thought of as some exotic escape for rich people, but it won't be that at all. For the [the pioneers] that go to Mars, it will be far more dangerous. But for those who go, opportunity awaits. There is going to be an explosion of entrepreneurial activity, because Mars will need everything from iron foundries to pizza joints," Musk said.

For the billionaire himself, that vision of building a new frontier as an explorer is part of a mindset that has fueled his success. It is the essence of what drives him to innovate and disrupt the status quo.

"I wake up every morning and think the future is going to be great, and that's what being a spacefaring civilization is about," Musk said. "It's about believing in the future and thinking that the future will be better than the past. And I can't think of anything more exciting than going out there and being among the stars."

As personal and unique as the definition of success may be, one thing is certain—most of us would like to believe we clearly recognize success when we see it. But do we really know the true meaning of success? There is little argument that an Olympic athlete has achieved success when she leans forward to accept a gold medal as it is draped around her neck, or when a team of climbers reaches the peak of a mountaintop, or when Elon Musk's SpaceX successfully launches and recovers the latest rocket. Each of these people have demonstrated fortitude and tenacity driven by the power of their convictions. These are indisputable achievements we clearly define as success, but is that it? Can success simply be summed up in one word—*achievement*?

Let's face it, goals equate to our ambitions. By definition, an ambition is something we desire that has not yet been achieved. While achievement certainly defines success, it is only one aspect of what we, as a society, have accepted as an *absolute* example of success.

The great Jim Rohn—entrepreneur, author, and motivational speaker—often defined success as "the slow and steady progress toward our dreams, goals, and aspirations." When we consider the power of Mr. Rohn's words, we begin to clearly see that success is so much more than achievement. In fact, success is not measured by an achievement inasmuch as it is measured by the growth and happiness acquired through a personal transformation, which takes place as we move toward our goals. It is an appreciation of life's journey as we *enjoy* the price of success rather than *paying* for it as we anticipate the promise of our future. It is, therefore, important to strike a balance between the importance of enjoying the journey—an appreciation or awareness of the present—with our desire to envision a better life for ourselves through the power of goals—our future.

Most successful people are visionaries. They think strategically. They are goal-oriented and goal-driven. That is *not* to say these people don't know how to enjoy the essence of the moment. In fact, it may be fair to say that the quality of each moment for these people is *enhanced* by the very nature of their ability to "see" both the future as well as the present moment.

Develop a Millionaire Mindset

A millionaire mindset describes an attitude characterized by a determination to reach a goal or create a lifestyle despite social status or current life circumstances. This mindset provides us with an ability to see past what *is* to what *is possible.*

Most people who say they want a million dollars actually want to *spend* a million dollars. Those who have a millionaire mindset appreciate the value of money and what it can do for them. They realize that if they're ever going to get anywhere close to amassing a million dollars (and the things it can do for them and others), they have to have the right mindset. Consider the approach most people take when they set up their savings strategy. They *first* set up their lives and *then* try to save after the fact, when it is convenient. By the way, it is never "convenient." This approach is a recipe for failure from the very start.

The millionaire mindset puts savings goals first with tried and true principles like paying yourself first, taking advantage of pay raises by setting aside some for savings, prudent investments, and smart tax strategies. After all, it's not so much about what you *make* but what you *keep* that matters in the grand scheme of finance.

Reaching a goal of this magnitude (wealth-related or not) requires clarity, conviction, and consistency. Your goal must be clear. Clarity draws a distinction to the purpose of your goal, which drives your conviction. Finally, you must consistently do everything it takes to make daily progress toward your goals if you ever expect to achieve them. This includes both action and your state of mind.

A Frame of Reference

The sad truth is, most people never become as financially successful as they could be. And they end up going through life never knowing why.

The subtleties of life often provide the most profound insight. For example, most people go about life seeing things as they are and subscribe to the "if only, then" mindset. Theirs is a point of view that "*if only* things were different, *then* I'd be happy," or "*if only* I could win the lottery, *then* I'd be able to live the kind of life I want." This mindset severely affects our power because of the limiting conditions it places upon our ability to change. Instead, we relegate that power to the circumstances of *if only*.

Instead of tying our own hands with such an approach, we should instead look for ways to gain control of our situation using a mindset that places us in better control of the direction and tempo of our lives. Using the "if only, then" approach compels us to consider all of the *external* factors that are working against us—the housing market, the stock market, gas prices, interest rates, a lack of time, or our circumstances. As a result, our frustrations lead us to wishful thinking, conjecture, and fantasies of somehow striking it rich with a winning lottery ticket or a windfall inheritance from someone we have never even heard of or barely know at all.

To a large extent, the root of the problem is not external at all. If it were, *no one* would be able to create wealth or achieve success to any great extent. Yet, time and again we see glaring examples of people who achieve great wealth and live happy lives *despite* external circumstance. How are *they* doing it?

One of the biggest obstacles to setting and achieving goals is our own self-limiting beliefs. The state of mind we choose to employ is a clear difference-maker when it comes to goal attainment. A lot of people set goals and immediately begin doubting their abilities the very next moment. These people tend to have a really bad habit of getting in their own way. As much as they desire to achieve their goals, they immediately begin focusing on their limitations rather than their strengths and attributes. These are areas where they believe themselves to be limited in some way.

You may have found yourself here a time or two. You begin by believing yourself to be inadequate or inferior in areas such as intelligence, ability, talent, creativity, personality, or something else. As a result, you sell yourself short. By underestimating yourself, you either set *no* goals, or *low* goals that are far below what you are truly capable of accomplishing. Your internal programming is then set to a default mode that focuses on inadequacies over abilities. To counteract this, you must begin by tapping into the power of why you even set goals to begin with.

Our thoughts, beliefs, and actions support our *why*. Our internal programming, along with the things we have learned over the years, create the lens we peer through to assess life. But what if we consciously choose to consider life from an alternate perspective—one offering a *wide-angle* perspective? Logic alone tells us we will see more. But is "more" better? When it comes to perspective, more is almost *always* better.

The clearer you can be about your long-term future, the more rapidly you will attract people, circumstances, and opportunities into your life to help make that future a reality. The greater clarity you have about who you are and what you want, the more you will achieve and the faster you will see it in every area of your life.

Create Your Own Future:

1. **Use the power of your imagination.** Imagine that there is a solution to every problem, a way to overcome every limitation, and no limit on your achieving every goal you can set for yourself. What would you do differently?

2. **Practice thinking in retrospect**. Project forward five years and look back to the present. What would have to have happened along the journey for your world to be ideal?

3. **Release self-imposed limitations.** Imagine your financial life to be perfect in every way. How much would you be earning? How much would you be worth? What steps could

you take, starting today, to make these goals a reality? Doing *nothing* assures *nothing* will change.

4. **Redefine your ideal life.** Imagine your family and personal life as perfect. What would it look like? What should you start doing more of, or less of, starting today in order to bring about that storyline?

5. **Work your plan and plan your work.** Plan your perfect calendar. Design your year from January to December as if you had no limitations. What would you change, starting today? How would you feel? Allow your excitement to drive you. What changes would you have to make to be able to live out your plan?

6. **Find the new you.** Imagine your health and fitness lifestyle to be perfect in every way. What is your weight? How do you feel? What could you do, starting today, to make the vision for yourself into a reality?

Goal-Setting – The Real Difference

Goal-Setting

Goal *setting* requires a person to visualize their ideal future self, surrounded by the conditions they desire. Learning the incredible power of goals can forever change your life. But, as we have learned so far, setting a goal requires a clear and actionable plan as to how something will be achieved. The absence of an actionable plan essentially reduces a goal to a wish, a hope, or a mere fleeting desire, which we all know will *never* fully materialize.

Setting goals requires us to formulate a crystal-clear vision—a mental picture—of the desires and conditions we wish to achieve.

A verbal declaration is a great start, but it does little to perpetuate the conditions that formulate the foundation for setting a goal. Declaring how you would like to lose weight or earn more money is not enough to provide the clarity required to set the framework of a goal.

Specificity is the *absolute* essential element in setting any goal. When you declare your goals, be specific. How much weight do you wish to lose? How much more money do you wish to make? If you can answer the five W's (*Who, What, Where, When,* and most importantly, *Why*) then you will have set a solid foundation upon which you can *set* your goals. As you contemplate each of the five W's, remove the limits you are naturally inclined to place upon yourself based on what you *think* you know about the limitations, obstacles, and variables you are likely to encounter. This is not the time nor the place to consider them, as it is not part of the goal *setting* process.

Once you figure out the WHY,
the HOW will reveal itself.

No Limitations

Imagine having all the time, talents, and abilities you could ever require to achieve any goal you set. No matter where you are in life, you have all the friends, contacts, resources, and advantages you need to seize every opportunity and achieve anything you desire. You have no limitations whatsoever on what you could be, have, or do in the pursuit of your dreams, hopes, desires…and goals. How do these ideal conditions make you feel? Encouraged? Motivated? Energized?

Whether you currently realize it or not, every one of the conditions above are *not* reserved for the "lucky" few who happen to have special powers or influence. You, too, can operate in these very same conditions. All you have to do is get out of your own way. And by that, I mean you must begin seeing the world differently. Doing so opens the door to an indescribable energy flow that actually *facilitates* these empowering conditions.

The difference between an open and closed energy flow is subtle but significant. This is where the final element in the Triple-S concept begins to become an increasingly important part of the equation. Without the third element of the Triple-S formula, we essentially have what amounts to a two-legged stool. It's a *good start* that will work, albeit with some limitations, but it's an incomplete solution. So, what if I told you that the third and final element will turn a *good* formula into a *great* formula that will work *every* time, *all* the time?

With an effective *strategy* in place that is constructed in alignment with our *story*, we set the conditions for success. To put that formula into high gear, we must be in the right *state*. Our *State* (the final element) is broadly defined as the *psychological, physiological*, and *emotional* condition we are in at any given time. Our state shapes our story and serves as a filter that determines how we see our lives. The filter of our state is divided into three overarching elements: our focus (or state of mind), our physiology (or physical state), and our awareness (or spiritual state). In essence, it is the balance of mind, body, and spirit that brings us into harmonious alignment with our "best self."

State of Mind

A balanced state of mind is evidenced by a clarity of purpose. Having a clear and undeniable purpose propels the mind into some pretty amazing places. It is in these places where creativity and imagination abound...a place where there are *no limits* and where visions of what is possible are revealed. Do not consider these encounters with imagination as insignificant. If your mind takes you to a place where your imagination takes control, be quick to take a back seat (by getting out of your own way) and observe the possibilities.

"Whatever the mind of man can conceive and believe, it can achieve."
~ Napoleon Hill

Okay, so we keep seeing the phrase, "Get out of your own way." So, what the heck does that really mean? And how do we actually go about doing it once we understand it?

Getting out of your own way is simply a way to remind you to be mindful of (and where possible, to eliminate) the internal struggle with what you have come to believe as limitations, and to begin embracing what is possible. Transform "I can't" to "I can." Replace pessimism with optimism. Substitute judgment for gratitude. Release any and all doubts about your abilities. They don't matter at this point. All that matters is the narrative your imagination is trying to rewrite by showing you what *is* possible.

Most people are unaware that the quality of their life is largely determined by their self-communication and ability to manage their states. The words we have running through our mind contribute to our story and reflect our state of mind. That state of mind is manifested externally by the words we speak and the attitudes we convey. By managing our language, we manage our emotions and our behaviors. If your internal default language is negative, it may be time for you to learn a new language.

Reprogram your mind with the elements that lead you to your purpose. Think about your typical daily routine for a moment. It's true that with any given day there are differences. There are also similarities. Focus for a moment on the similarities of your typical daily routine. What are some of the rituals you go through every single day? List them on paper or on the computer if it makes it easier to examine. Once this small task is complete, take a look at every ritual and strike through the ones that don't provide value to your purpose. Too much television, computer/social media/video games?

Pay close attention to the things you feed your mind on a daily basis that is actually counterproductive to reaching your goals and objectives. A simple realignment may be just what you need to reach a balanced state of mind. WARNING: Just because the word "simple" is used does not mean that making the change will be easy…unless you have *resolved* to change your conditions to meet the story narrative leading to your goal.

"Where energy goes, focus flows."
~ *Tony Robbins*

The direction and momentum of our lives are largely determined by what we choose to focus on. That is principally why we must be mindful to focus on our goal and not on what we fear. Resist fear in *all* areas. A determined focus invigorates the drive and tenacity required to overcome fear and circumstance. It is a difference-maker that serves to distinguish the winners from the quitters.

Physiological State

Our state of mind is intrinsically connected to our physiology. In fact, the two are so closely related that a slight change in one can lead to significant changes in the other. Physiology is a broad term used to describe:

- Body movements
- Gestures
- Posture
- Eye-gaze or focus
- Breathing and heart rate
- Muscle tension
- Facial expression

The same blood that flows through your body also flows through your brain. If you don't take care of your body, your neglect will eventually affect your mind, and if you don't take care of your mind, it will eventually affect your body. There is no getting away from this reciprocating fundamental truth. The point is, we must be consciously aware of the things we are doing to promote the health and wellness of both our mind and our body if we are to expect peak performance of ourselves to any extent. One of the best ways to do that is through proper nutrition, regular exercise, and spiritual awareness. If we are physically fit, we become more aware. If we are aware, then we are awake. And if we are awake, then we are alive!

It has been said that emotion is created by motion. In other words, you can *instantly* change your emotions by *doing* something. Part of the *doing* is evidenced in the way we carry ourselves (posture, facial expression, and breathing). Try it. Next time you're feeling less than yourself, adjust your posture. Put your shoulders back, lift your chin, and take a few deep breaths. I promise you will feel the difference these slight adjustments make in your ability to think clearer, make better decisions, and experience a sense of clarity. Go ahead…give it a try right now.

Movement is key to changing your state. The way you move changes the way you feel. It is the one thing you can do to *immediately* change your state. So, make it a goal to become more aware of your physiology as it applies to your health, your social interaction, and your influence with others. These changes will bring about a profound effect on the goals and objectives you have set for your life.

Spiritual State

Our spiritual state is most closely aligned to an intangible connection we have with awareness—a force, or source, *greater* than our self. Awareness leads to insight, which leads to introspection. This introspection is a self-awareness we gain by examining our own mental and emotional thought processes.

Whether they know it or not, people change states several times throughout any given day. They are happy, angry, judgmental, cynical, hopeful, kind, etc. Not only is this counterproductive, it confuses the subconscious. As a result, these people end up going in circles instead of proceeding on a *laser* course to their goals and objectives. If this describes you, then stop the madness by getting ahold of your competing states through awareness, and then take *action* to change things. Ridding ourselves of counterproductive behaviors places us in alignment with a state of peak performance. Peak performance comes from being in peak state.

We can change our state in an instant, and in so doing, we can change the moment, the hour, or our entire life. A change in state requires only our decision. That's the beautiful simplicity of the power we have over the course of our lives. The only precursor to our decision is an *awareness* that our state requires an adjustment. Think of it more like a light switch. Once you become aware of the need for an adjustment, you simply turn on the switch and *BAM!*... you put yourself in a state of peak performance. This places you squarely in a state of readiness to address virtually any issue.

Here is an encouraging declaration: You have the power to achieve every goal you set as long as you are in a state of readiness and you *act* upon an effective strategy of achievement. Excellent! So...how do we know if it is an *effective strategy*?

Begin with the End in Mind

Every one of us is programmed to look forward. In other words, we are programmed with a desire to achieve, become, or obtain something "more" in our lives, no matter how little or how great. As a child, every one of us had a dream to *become* something when we "grew up." Think back for a moment to some of the things you dreamed you would be doing at this point in your life. Are you anywhere close to the ideals and objectives you set for yourself? Are you at least *on track* to achieving your goals? If so, great. If not, uh-oh... an adjustment is in order.

One of the things we must consider as we drive toward our goal is an effective strategy. Our strategy is driven by our ability to clearly define a path to achievement. The path and the methods we use to navigate that path serve as our strategy—the things we must do in order to bring about our goal.

Looking forward toward a goal or objective may be difficult at first. We are uncertain as to the process or steps we must take to bring about our goals. So, we end up "doing our best" as we travel a path we believe will lead us to the realization of our goals. But what if there is a better way?

Once we have established a crystal-clear vision of just what we desire as our goal, we are able to visit that vision frequently and with increasing ease. The more we envision the goal, the more ingrained it becomes in our subconscious mind. Once our subconscious mind is convinced that the vision is the new reality, you will find yourself taking actions that support the natural attraction of your vision.

With our goal firmly on the side of our most familiar and intimate thoughts comes an ability to "project our self" into a state of mind that allows us to virtually experience every aspect of what it will be like once we have fully achieved the goal. Our imagination provides a powerful advantage to immerse ourselves into a full spectrum of the goal, even to the point where we are able to "look back" upon the things it took for us to achieve it. It is this *backward look* that is an extremely powerful tool in the arsenal of our ability to gain clarity and create an action plan of achievement toward the very goal in which we are virtually immersed.

Goal-Getting

The principle element of the goal-getting process is *action*. Once you develop the ability to effectively *set* your goals, you put into motion a process that awakens the winner inside of you. FAIR WARNING: Once the winner emerges, you should prepare for real and lasting change to come about as you discover the *actions* you will be compelled to take that bring your goals to reality. Once the winner emerges, you will have difficulty refusing its call to action without a lot of consternation…quite simply because *now* you know the way and are *compelled* to act.

Goal-getting compels us to give serious consideration to the habits and rituals we have and to evaluate whether they have a positive or negative influence on our ability to achieve the goals we have set for our life. Your daily rituals are *vitally* important in the processes you employ to achieve your goals. The determination of a successful outcome is in direct proportion to your commitment to put the proper rituals and habits into the process of your plan for achievement.

Every action you take is rooted in volition—the power of using one's will. That is, there is a goal behind it. The most basic goal—to take another breath—and the most profound—self-discovery—are both attained through action. Remember that, because *action* is the *only* path to goal attainment, including the ultimate goal—the attainment of happiness. We'll dive deeper into the goal-getting process in the second half of this book. For now, your fundamental understanding and awareness that *action* is the catalyst of achievement will prepare you for what you will learn in the latter half.

Some Final Thoughts

➤ **Develop a Millionaire Mindset.** Most people are not millionaires because they don't think like millionaires. In fact, those who have yet to achieve this milestone typically equate the status solely to money. Those who have developed a millionaire mindset have something far more valuable than money will ever be able to buy—insight. Theirs is a total mindset leading to what is truly valuable in life—balance, leading to an enriched life supported by happiness.

➤ **Create Your Own Future.** When you dream of the future, does your mind paint a picture of something you actually *believe* will happen? As you imagine the kind of life you desire, are you using the full capacity of your imagination? Have you made certain to remove all limitations? If not, what are the elements preventing you from fully embracing the idea that *everything* is possible? An ability to identify your current limitations is a powerful first step in the changes you desire. Your current circumstances are relevant only to the extent that they reveal conditions you are initially up against. Every obstacle can be overcome. Expertise can be acquired. The power to shape your future begins with a recognition of the obvious and the magic of your imagination. See everything, feel everything, taste everything, smell everything…and prepare to savor the reality of it all.

➤ **Goal-Setting.** You can begin enjoying the achievement of your goal well before you physically attain it. Your subconscious is fertile ground for planting the seeds of imagination. As your imagination paints the ideal picture of your goal, be quick to remove the limitations that prevent you from the entirety of the full experience of your goal. A subconscious mind that is well fed by an active imagination creates a state of mind that is prepared for everything it has been programmed to receive. A balanced mind, body, and spirit provides the conditions that allow us to seize the moment when reality crosses paths with imagination—that very point where preparation meets opportunity.

> **Begin with the End in Mind.** The projection of a forward-thinking mindset can be helpful as you lay out the roadmap leading to your goals. Allow your subconscious mind to immerse you into the full experience of a completed goal. Take a virtual assessment of your surroundings, from the clothes you're wearing to the people and places that surround you. Then, turn around and take a critical look back at the path that brought you to this point. Look for the things that had to occur in order for your goal to materialize. Write down the things you see that you must do in order to bring this vision to reality. Then…take action!

Thought-provoking questions…

1. Our convictions provide a foundation of courage, allowing us to prevail against obstacles and difficulties that will inevitably appear in our life from time to time. Have you developed the kind of determination that drives a deep-seeded conviction to achieve your dreams, goals, and aspirations? Have you taken ownership of bringing your future to reality, or are you satisfied with a reactive mindset?

2. The subtleties of life often provide the most profound insight. Are you aware of those subtleties? If so, you're off to a fantastic start. If not, you're missing a key element in the formula for achievement. For, even if you do succeed, you will likely not fully appreciate it.

3. Are you getting in your own way? Do you second-guess your own motivations or place your goals subordinate to the sensitivities of others? If so, perhaps it's time you consider another approach. Eliminate self-limiting beliefs that disguise themselves as honorable humility. Give yourself permission to boldly step forward and declare your willingness to be the recipient of overwhelming avalanches of abundance!

Chapter Six

Discover Your Purpose

*"The two most important days in your life
are the day you were born,
and the day you find out why."*
~ *Mark Twain*

We exist on this earth for a finite period of time. During that
time, we make decisions and choices that shape our individual lives. In fact, we are summarily *defined* by our decisions and
choices. Contrary to popular belief, life doesn't just happen. You,
or someone or some*thing* around you, influences your thoughts,
beliefs, and actions. How you react to those influences—whether
you elect to allow someone or something else make the choices *for
you*—determines how you develop as an individual. Our reactions
(thoughts, beliefs, and actions) determine how we treat other people,
the level of education we attain, who we marry, what we do in our
career, and what we ultimately achieve in life—the entirety of which
influences whether we discover the true essence of our purpose.

Every one of us has a purpose. To find your purpose, you are well
advised to stop looking and start doing. The best results are realized

by taking *action* toward your goals and to begin trying new things. By taking action you attract people, opportunities, ideas, inspiration, and resources into your life that help you move toward your goal—and your purpose—more efficiently. Each of these elements plays a significant role in helping you discover your purpose. A goal driven by purpose helps us to create an *intentional* goal. Intentional goals are clear, concise, specific, and powerful.

> *I realized my purpose was to be a writer…once I started writing.*

Many people become frustrated because they try to find that one thing they are meant to do; but trying to find one thing is primarily the reason we get so frustrated. The notion that we have only one thing we're destined to do limits us from the full experience of life and the fulfillment we seek in knowing our purpose. It may turn out that there is indeed one overarching "thing" that defines your purpose. And if that's the result, embrace it. However, there is room for argument that your purpose is not a "thing" at all, but rather, a theme. Your purpose could very well be a theme that leads you to discover many things along the journey of your life that you can be passionate about as you live your life's purpose.

Tap into the Power of Your Passions

Far too many of us lose sight of our passions for the sake of discovering our purpose. If we will make a choice to *live* our passions, we will be more likely to discover the true nature of our purpose. When you lead a passionate life, you are leading a life of purpose. And when you're leading a life of purpose, you are operating in the flow of life, placing yourself in direct alignment with where you are supposed to be.

When you feel disconnected from life, you lack purpose and passion. To fix this, follow the leading of your passions. Go all in. Immerse yourself in *every* aspect of your passions. Savor the essence of everything involving your passion and reconnect with life. Your action and activity will reinvigorate you and reveal how the true purpose of life is to be fully involved in living.

As your purpose emerges—and it *will* emerge—it will resonate with you so deeply that it will stir emotions within you that confirm the magnitude of your discovery. Your revelation will be so real that it will be the first thing you think about in the morning and the last thing you think of at night. Knowing your purpose activates your subconscious mind and begins to change the essence of your story—the narrative you live by. Any thought, plan, goal, or action supported by the influence of your purpose reprograms the narrative that you define in your conscious mind. This new narrative will immediately begin to reshape the conditions of your life by the actions you take in response to the new perspective or outlook you have on life.

A Fresh New Mindset

A purpose-filled life empowers you with greater insight, awareness, and enthusiasm, providing you with a distinct advantage over those who are still waiting on their purpose to come to them. *Action* opens the pathways leading to your purpose, helping you to become increasingly aware of opportunity before most other people. Therefore, in order for change or progress to occur, you must *do* something. Action brings awareness to all kinds of opportunities and possibilities that have everything to do with finding your purpose.

Okay, so if *action* is the key, what *action* should you take? Answer: Any action that speaks to your "Why." A quick recap of our *why* reminds us that we are driven to act—in large part—by fear and desire; that is, by what we have to lose and what we have to gain. However, there is one other aspect I highly recommend you factor in to the equation of your why—generosity. All too often, we get so caught up in the competing forces of fear (loss) and desire (gain) that we fail to consider what we have to *give*. The spirit of generosity is so closely related to the emotional epicenter of the human spirit that, assuming you can effectively harness it, it will help you overcome most any impeding condition or circumstance that leads you directly to your purpose. It will also bring you a great deal of satisfaction, fulfillment, and joy. In other words, you'll know you're on the right track by the way you feel and the manner in which things begin to happen for you, not to mention the affect you will have on the lives of others.

Speaking of others...many of your choices stretch beyond an immediate affect to your own life and influence the lives of others. Of all the choices you make, those that have an effect beyond your own life bring you the most meaning and begin to shape the essence of who you are. Consider the following story as a case in point.

This evening I joined my dad for dinner at one of his favorite restaurants. He ordered a lot more food than he typically does and only ended up eating half of it. On the drive home, he took an unfamiliar route. Curious, I decided to watch things play out. Soon after, he parked the car near an alley and said, "I'll be right back." He grabbed the leftovers, ran into the alley, and returned empty-handed. When I asked him what just happened, he replied, "There's a homeless guy back there who I've been helping out for the last year or so."

As you do things that increasingly bring you satisfaction and fulfillment, you will have most of what you need for an action plan and can then begin setting goals to achieve milestones that reveal the answers and conditions you seek. Your actions will begin to reveal information, education, and insight supporting your purpose. You may very well find yourself in the company of an entirely new circle of people who think on the same level as you engage in conversations supporting your goals and aspirations. It may seem coincidental at first, but it is far from coincidence, I assure you. Opportunity, not coincidence, is connected to a purpose-driven life. Opportunity will bring you fresh ideas and information that can be leveraged to support the very goals you have set for the discovery of your purpose and the fulfillment of your dreams.

> *"Attention is the key to life. Whatever you give your attention to, you become. Whatever you concentrate upon will come into your life. We grow into the thing that fills our thoughts as inevitably as the stream merges into the ocean at last."*
> ~ Emmet Fox

The quote above, by Emmet Fox, teaches us that wherever our attention goes, our life goes as well. When we discover our purpose, our level of awareness grows as we become increasingly sensitive to everything in our environment that can help us to achieve goals related to our purpose.

Built on Purpose

Your purpose has everything to do with your goals, but your goals do not always have everything to do with your purpose. For clarity, let's reexamine the fundamental definition of a goal. A goal is an aspiration, an object, or condition of your desire to accomplish, achieve, or receive. Goals are designed for a reason or purpose. However, goals are not always of your own making; you may be influenced, manipulated, or forced to pursue a goal, and as such, those goals will have little—if anything—to do with fulfilling your life's purpose. Fortunately, personal goals are self-derived, driven by an intent to reach a desired end state that *does* indeed support personal growth leading to a purpose.

You may be goal-oriented—that is, you are *driven* by goals—or you may have just a few goals, or you may not think much about goals at all. Wherever you fall in the broad spectrum of goal orientation, it is safe to assume you have an interest in learning more about goals or you wouldn't be reading this book.

Goals are *always* based on the future. Once a goal has been accomplished, it is no longer a goal, but an achievement. Purpose, on the other hand, is a dynamic and enduring condition that always resides in the *present moment,* reflecting not only who you are today but who you become in the future. The principle fascination with purpose is its ability to change and adapt over time, hence its enduring characteristics. But it is the very nature of that character that brings the highest value to our life—true meaning by way of a lifelong contribution.

One of the greatest gifts is to know our purpose. Knowing our purpose reminds us of the value each and every one of us has in this life. It also reminds us that the present moment—right now—is all we truly have. So, savor the moments as you live your purpose!

"There is one quality which one must possess to win, and that is definiteness of purpose, the knowledge of what one wants, and a burning desire to possess it."
~ *Napoleon Hill*

Make It Personal

Your intense, burning desire is an absolute essential ingredient to the attainment of your goals. Your motivation must be more than desire. It must be a desire so intense that it is capable of overcoming inevitable obstacles you are bound to encounter along the way to achievement. For your desire to be intense enough, your goals *must* be personal. They must be goals that *you* choose for yourself, rather than goals someone else wants for you, or ones you want to achieve to be *like* someone else.

For the goal process to be effective, you must be selfish about what it is that you really want for yourself. This doesn't mean that you shouldn't do things for other people. It simply means that, in setting goals for your life, you should start with yourself. After all, only when you are at your best can you *give* your best to others. Therefore, you must...

Decide What You *Really* Want

➤ What are your three most important financial goals?

➤ What are your three most important health and fitness goals?

➤ What are your three most important business and career goals?

➤ What are your three most important family or relationship goals?

It is important for us to keep things in perspective. Although it would be great if we could ignore this part, the truth remains that we live in a world full of obstacles and hurdles. So, it is wise for us to ask the right questions when it comes to considering the reality of it all. With that in mind, here are some questions for you to consider as you approach the goal-setting process.

➢ What are your three biggest worries or concerns in life, right now?

➢ What bothers you, preoccupies you, or distracts you in your day-to-day life?

➢ What aggravates or irritates you?

➢ What is robbing you of joy, more than anything else?

Once you have identified your biggest problems, worries, or concerns, ask yourself:

➢ What are the ideal solutions to each of these problems?

➢ How can I reduce or eliminate these problems or worries immediately?

➢ What is the fastest and most direct way to solve each of these problems?

Every question we ask in the goal-setting and getting process is important. In fact, every question in life we ask is important. Questions open the door to answers. Your questions *will* be answered. Your responsibility, once they are answered, will be to respond in a manner that brings you closer to the life you seek and desire.

"The simplest and most direct solution, requiring the fewest number of steps, is usually the correct solution to any problem."
~ William of Ockham, British philosopher

Keep It Simple

Many people make the mistake of over-complicating goals and problems. But the more complicated the solution, the less likely that solution will ever be attempted, and the longer it will take to get any results. Your objective should be to simplify the solution and go directly to the goal, as quickly as possible.

For example, people often tell me how they would love to write a book. If they are truly sincere, I ask them how they plan to go about getting it done. After we discuss things from their perspective, I give them what I consider to be the best answer:

Sit down and write!

The simplest, most direct way to write a book has always been and continues to be the same—spend time writing. Spend enough time writing and most anyone can create enough content to write a book. If you don't upgrade your writing skills or change anything else about what you are doing beyond making sure you spend enough time writing, every day, you will most likely have enough words written to publish a book. And so it goes with virtually every facet of our lives when it comes to accomplishment. Far too many people fall short of establishing or relating to the goal because they are focusing on the *work* required to get them there.

Connecting Your Goals to Your Purpose

One way to leverage your goals is to ensure they align with your purpose. Even if you don't yet know your purpose, you can still leverage your goals by connecting them to your passions. One very effective way to do that is by putting your goals in writing. Here is an exercise you can do that is both easy and insightful.

1. Take out a sheet of paper and write down a list of ten goals you would like to accomplish. Write each of them in the present tense, as though you had already achieved these goals. For example, "I currently weigh ____ pounds." Or, "I earn $____ per year." "I live in the house of my dreams. It is located in _____." This present-tense methodology does something very powerful. It begins to convince the subconscious mind that your goal has already materialized. This mindset empowers you with a sense of accomplishment the likes of which prepares you to receive the abundance that is already on its way to you.

2. Connect each of your goals to an emotion. For example, "I currently weigh ____ pounds and that gives me greater *confidence.*" Or, "I earn $_____ per year and *I'm happy* I can now afford to (help more people, buy a new home, pay for college tuition, etc.)." Pay close attention to how these declarations make you feel. This is the *psychological or emotional connection process.* Leverage this aspect of the process and you will dramatically increase your chances for a successful achievement.

3. Describe each of your goals in detail. What do they look like, what do they smell like, what color, style, shape, or form do they have? This is the *physical connection process,* which is second in power only to the emotional connection you have with your goals.

4. Once you have completed your list of ten goals, review the list. Allow your mind to absorb each of the goals you have written, taking special care not to overanalyze things yet. This is *the reflection process.* Remember, it is your mind that created each one of the goals in the first place. The reflection process allows your mind to "see" the goals as they are reflected from a place other than the confines of your mind.

This process ignites a fascinating course of action that begins to convince the subconscious mind of your intentions. Recall that intentional goals are clear, concise, specific...and extremely powerful.

Once you have allowed your mind to pore over the goals you have created, ask yourself the following questions:

1. What *one* goal on this list, if I were to accomplish it immediately, would have the greatest positive impact on my life?

2. How would the accomplishment of this one goal *change* my life and/or the lives of others?

3. What action (or actions) do I need to take to begin making progress toward this goal?

With your mind focused on your one primary goal, write down everything you can think of that you can *do* to achieve it, then create an action list focused solely on that one goal. Then take *action* on this specific goal *every single day* for thirty days. Here are some action recommendations for you to consider:

1. **Research** (knowledge, insight, education, investigation, etc.)

2. **Write** (business plans, financial plans, construction plans, outlines, correspondence, etc.)

3. **Collaborate** (partnerships, teams, groups, etc.)

4. **Communicate** (mentors, coaches, bankers, accountants, attorneys, contractors, etc.)

5. **Invest** (money, time, energy)

Write your goal on a 3 x 5 index card (old school) or put it in your phone and carry it with you. Review it regularly. Think about this goal morning, noon, and night. Continually look for ways to achieve it by asking one very powerful overarching question:

How?

> **"How long should you try?**
> **Until."**
> ~ *Jim Rohn*

Okay, so we have established that your passions lead to your purpose, and we have established that you must *act* on those passions in order to begin the process that will inevitably lead you to your life's purpose. There's one thing left for you to do…

Enjoy the Journey

Think of someone you really enjoy being around. Quick, what was the first thing you envisioned as you thought of this person? Was it their smiling face, their laughter, the carefree nature they have? Have you ever stopped to wonder how they can be so joyous most of the time? What's their secret?

Now think about the way you *feel* when you're around this person. I believe what you *see* is only a small part of what you actually discern. What you *feel* is far more significant. While it is certainly true that you're attracted to the outward signs of joy, you are *drawn in* by what that joy creates for you on a deeper level. You see, these people have discovered that the secret to a more satisfying and fulfilling life on every level is to create joy for others.

"Joy comes when you accept who you are,
why you are, and how you are
in the process of becoming."
~ Andy Andrews

The journey to find our purpose should be one we enjoy. Enjoyment brings about a sense of peace that allows us to transcend the volatility of life, even while others are struggling to make sense of it all. Enjoyment instills a joyous nature. A joyous nature is attractive. It attracts hope, certainty, sincerity, kindness, and goodness. People are drawn to joy because of the way it makes *them* feel. Joy connects on an emotional and spiritual level to unite and inspire. I happen to be married to a woman who is one of the most joyous people I have ever known. Others feel the same about her and are attracted to the way she makes them feel because of the joy she finds in nearly every facet of life.

Joy is a choice. In just about any situation, you will find what you're looking for. Look, I get it, life can be difficult. It can also be fantastic. Whether it is difficult or whether it absolutely sucks, the choice of how you frame it is yours alone. Why not choose to look for the good in *every* situation? There is always good to be found. *Enjoy* the journey of your life, and your life will show you reasons to be joyous. It may even reveal the purpose it has for you along the way.

One of the best ways to find joy is to embrace gratitude. Gratitude is thought to be the most important key to success. Gratitude drives your decision-making and increases your productivity. An account of all we are grateful for brings us into alignment with what is truly important in life. Consider the fact that, as you read this, you are alive—the ultimate reason to be joyous. If you are healthy, have a roof over your head, money to buy the essentials, and people in your life, you have every reason to be even *more* joyous.

Joy is a matter of perspective. I have often said that if you can change your perspective you can change your life. For example, instead of accepting the fact that you must *pay* a price for success and achievement, why not instead choose to find ways to *enjoy* the price? By putting some thought here, you can always find ways to enjoy the process, which is actually the preferred method of goal achievement. After all, if you don't enjoy the process, you won't be willing to do whatever it takes to achieve your goals when disruption or conflict arises.

Here are some things to consider regarding the perspective of your goals in finding your purpose and joy in the process.

Consider the one thing you would do—right now—to reach your goal if you knew you would not fail. Go back to your list of ten goals. Make sure each of them are framed in the present tense. Review the one goal from that list that would have the greatest positive impact on your life and immediately take action on it. Consider the varying perspectives of the effects that goal will have on you and others close to you. Determine how you will measure the progress and success in achieving this goal. Do something every day to reel that goal in closer and closer. Be grateful for what you have and for what you are aware of. Celebrate the milestones you achieve along the path to your objectives.

Review your goals every day. Take action on at least *one* thing immediately. Imagine the opportunities you will have to enjoy the price of success in terms of additional work, time, commitment, and lifestyle rituals you must master to achieve your goal, and then get busy enjoying that price.

Some Final Thoughts

> ➢ **Tap into the power of your passions.** Live your life… passionately! Don't get so caught up in discovering your purpose that you ignore your passions. Your purpose will reveal itself as long as you are living your passions. By acting on your passions, you open the door to opportunities that would not otherwise have occurred. The things you enjoy

doing reconnect you with life and hold the clues to your life purpose.

> **Keep it simple.** A clearly defined goal makes it easier for us to devise a simple action plan to achievement. Very often, the simple approach holds the most promise for us in terms of goal accomplishment. Think in broad terms at first, then begin by breaking down each step you must do in order for your goal to be accomplished.

> **Enjoy the journey.** Far too many people are so preoccupied with "getting there" that they overlook what is right in front of them at that very moment. Life is not supposed to be complicated, yet we choose to complicate it anyway. Embrace gratitude. Doing so empowers you with insight on a level that connects you with infinite wisdom and places you into alignment with forces that bring about opportunities and joy.

Thought-provoking questions...

1. Where are you, right now? Your answer to this question defines the reality you have created for yourself to this point in life. Do you believe you have the power to re-shape it? If so, great! If not, why not?

2. What must you *do* to get from where you are to where you want to be? Action is the only way we change *what is* to *what will be*. Start living your passions today.

3. Are you a joyous person? Do you look for joy in most every situation? Do you look for the best in other people? Are you optimistic or pessimistic? Do you project joy in your narrative, tone, and posture? As you transform into joy, you

will attract opportunity into your life. Be intentional in your approach to life. It will return exactly what you demand of it. Seize opportunity when you see it, and opportunity will reward you handsomely!

4. Are you enjoying the journey of life or dreading the next moment because your life "sucks?" Embrace gratitude and watch your frame of reference transform before your very eyes.

Chapter Seven

Write Your Own Story

*"Your intuition knows what to write,
so get out of the way."*
~ Ray Bradbury

While it is true many things in our life are out of our ability to control, it is equally true that we are very much *in* control of the narrative we create in response to what happens around us. Life has a way of doing its best to convince us that we have little choice but to "go with the flow" and accept the ruse of reality. Sadly, most people accept the narrative of circumstance and live life well below their capabilities. To make matters worse, these same people begin making *choices* that fit a narrative of circumstance rather than one *they* write. What does all this have to do with goals? Everything.

Most people set goals based on the story they have created for their life. If you're setting goals based on a life of circumstantial acceptance, then you're well short of where you *could* be in terms of expectations and possibilities, not to mention achievement. In other words, you deserve so much more. So, why not *have* more?

If you're setting goals based upon a sound narrative where achievement is not limited by circumstance, then the story you have created is likely one in which you believe *more* is not only possible but certain. However, if circumstance is still a leading character in your story, change is in order. Instead of giving circumstance the leading role, find ways to write a story where circumstance is continually overcome by the powerful forces of determination and tenacity, allowing *achievement* and *expectation* to dominate the narrative. As you do, the story of your life will begin to fit a different narrative—one *you* define as you begin to realize the power you truly have to bring about a life of abundance through a well-written story.

The only person who can change the effects of your circumstances is…you. The way you go about doing that is to change the narrative of your story. As a published author, I enjoy the absolute control I have over the elements of writing. I can literally write anything I desire in any style or form in any given genre. I can be opinionated, dramatic, creative, inspirational, or downright controversial if I so choose. As the author of your own life story, you have the same full creative license to write *any* narrative you wish. There are no limitations.

Changing your story requires only your creative imagination and a perspective that keeps *you* (your biases and old, worn-out narrative) from getting in the way. Just think of the possibilities. When faced with adversity or obstacles, we can choose a *transformative* narrative instead of one that accepts defeat. We can choose VICTORY over defeat. We can choose LIFE over existence. We can develop a leading character (you) who has an optimistic outlook, attractive qualities, good fortune, keen insight, awareness, superior powers, etc. In other words, we can literally write a storyline to our advantage by saying "No!" to circumstance and "Yes!" to everything we desire for our lives. Consciously adopting this narrative opens the door to everything that awaits us.

"Belief creates the actual fact."
~ *William James*

Sometimes we have to work on our perspective because we have developed a narrow outlook on life. A narrow outlook is evidenced by a life encumbered by circumstance. So, if this describes the current condition of *your* life, rest assured, there are ways to overcome it. Changing our perspective changes the outlook we have on life. Here are some effective ways to do just that…

Change Your Outlook, Change Your Life

The way you see the world reflects your reality. The content and quality of your reality is directly connected to how you see yourself "fitting in" to the greater overall construct or picture of life. If you don't like your reality, change it. The fastest way to change your reality is through education, awareness, and action. The more you know about any given topic, the better informed you are. The more informed you are, the better you are at making choices and decisions that serve the intent of your goals and objectives. One of the very *best* methods to educate yourself is the practice of learning all you can about…*You.*

You have more control of the way you fit in to life than you realize. That may go against everything you have been taught over the years, but it is as true a statement as it is absolute. You see, as stated in previous chapters, how we fit in to life is determined by our values, beliefs, and actions. Our *values* drive the way we think. Our thoughts (*beliefs*) affect our choices and decisions and largely determine the *actions* we take in every imaginable situation. So, how do we gain better control of this process? Quite simply, we must get to know ourselves (and the world around us) better.

115

Personal development is one of the very best ways to better understand ourselves. Personal development sources increase the educational perspective we have by enhancing personal growth and increasing overall awareness. The more we know, the more aware we become. The more aware we are, the greater clarity we develop. Clarity has a profound effect on the values, beliefs, and actions we embrace. Our values affect what we believe to be possible. Once we believe something is possible, the only thing left for us to do is...*act!*

Carpe Diem!

Translated from its Latin origin, *Cape Diem* means *seize the day*. It is a powerful aphorism that reminds us all to take *action*. Of all our dreams, goals, plans, and well-intentions, none can materialize without action. Our good intentions can end up being a perpetual cycle of apathy and restlessness unless...we wake up to break the cycle and seize control by taking action to declare *now* as the time to take advantage of opportunity. Action is the precursor to accomplishment. Taking action isn't always pretty or perfect, but the alternative is to remain stuck in circumstances that separate us from our dreams, goals, and aspirations.

Time is the great equalizer. It does not discriminate. It does not care about winners and losers, excuses, fairness, or equality. You cannot "save" time in a traditional sense. The only way to manipulate time is to make the very best of every moment. Time presents an opportunity but demands a sense of urgency. Whatever your dream, goal, desire, or objective, start now! Every moment you wait is an opportunity that expires. After all, although we know precisely when our personal clock started, we don't know when it will end. So...Carpe Diem!

*A year from now, that time will have
passed. You will either be happy you
took action or wish you had.*

We judge ourselves by what we perceive to be the limits of our capabilities (self-image), while others judge us by our accomplishments (evidenced by what they see). Each perspective contains a hidden aspect that prevents full access to a complete awareness that is essential in knowing the truth.

Your self-image has a direct influence on your level of performance and effectiveness in all you do. It is about how you think and evaluate yourself at any given moment. This includes the labels you use to define yourself, your personality, and capabilities. It also includes the beliefs you have about how the external world perceives you. If you perceive the world is against you, you will work to protect and preserve what you have obtained. But if you perceive the world to be full of hope, opportunity, and the cooperation of others, you cannot help but act in the interest of your dreams, goals, and objectives, because your every expectation will be one of victory.

Buyer Beware

The beliefs you have about yourself are largely *subjective*, hence, they are often not based on reliable facts at all. Your beliefs are the result of information you have processed, interpreted, and internalized throughout your life. Your beliefs have been shaped and formed by everything from your early childhood, parents, and friends to the books you have read and the life experiences you have had. Therefore, it is important to note that your self-image is unreliably-based on perceived reality. In fact, more times than not, your self-image is diametrically different from the perceptions others have of you. So, your self-image has no basis in reality at all (nor does theirs by the way). Whether your self-image is anywhere near accurate or made up of *erroneous* beliefs, as far as you are concerned, your perspective represents the facts, and you will think, feel, and act accordingly. The greater point here is, if *reality* is so dynamic, why not create a reality where your dreams, goals, and aspirations can thrive? Just be mindful not to constrain your reality by your own limited perspective.

The worst of all beliefs are *self-limiting beliefs*. If you believe yourself to be inadequate or limited in some way (talent, skills, abilities, intellect), whether or not your belief is accurate, it becomes a truth by which you live. Once you believe it, you will adopt it as your reality and *act* as if you are deficient in that particular area of your life. Overcoming self-limiting beliefs and self-imposed limitations is often the *biggest obstacle* standing between you and the realization of your potential.

There are a number of factors that affect our self-image. One of the most influential stems from the environment in which you spend most of your time, where other people dwell. The actions and opinions of other people often influence how you feel about yourself and can be some of the strongest influences of your life. Rejection, judgment, ridicule, criticism, praise, encouragement, and acknowledgement all play a role in determining what you believe about yourself, your abilities, and the world around you. So, be careful who you associate with. They can have *everything* to do with the differences between victory and defeat, happiness and misery, success and failure.

Self-limiting beliefs can hold you back for years. However, if your story narrative is strong enough, you will not buy into these convincing narratives easily. A strong personal story builds convictions (beliefs) and determination that overcome such influences. Therefore, it is important to recognize self-limiting beliefs and to take action to eliminate them as soon as possible.

Almost every one of us has had an experience of mastering a skill in an area where we previously had no ability. Oftentimes, in hindsight, we realize just how our limiting self-image in that area was never based on reality at all. Each time we master a skill or gain insight to something compelling, we prove to ourselves that we have the ability to grow and begin to realize there really *are* no limits to the potential we have. Remove self-limiting beliefs and watch the story of your life unfold like a well-designed novel where the good guys consistently win!

Things Are Not Always What They Seem

According to an article in *Fortune* magazine on learning disabilities in business, many influential people—significant contributors to the world—were diagnosed in adolescence as being not particularly bright or capable. But by virtue of hard work, determination, and sheer tenacity, many went on to achieve great success in their profession and industry.

Benjamin Franklin dropped out of school at age ten because his parents could only afford to keep him in school until his tenth birthday. That didn't stop him from pursuing his education, however. He taught himself through voracious reading, answering the call of his unquenchable curiosity, and eventually went on to invent the lightning rod, the glass harmonica, and bifocals, among other things. And, as we now know, he also became one of America's Founding Fathers.

Richard Branson has dyslexia. Branson was a self-described "pretty bad student"—he didn't get good marks, and he did poorly on standardized tests. Instead of giving up, he used the power of his personality to drive him to success. Today, Branson, known for developing Virgin Records, Virgin Airlines, and many of its more technologically advanced spinoffs, is one of the richest people in the United Kingdom.

Author **Stephen King's** first novel was rejected thirty times. If it weren't for King's wife, the book *Carrie* may not have ever existed. After being consistently rejected by publishing houses, King gave up and threw his first book in the trash. His wife, Tabitha, retrieved the manuscript and urged King to finish it. To date, King's books have sold over 350 million copies and many of his books have been made into major motion pictures as well as television series.

As I have often said time and again, things are not always what they seem. Given that well-served mantra, circumstances tend to convince us of a false reality and can often lead us astray very quickly. Stories like these have been repeated thousands of times. These famous people are famous not because of some pre-ordained destiny but because each of them chose to write their own story despite the odds. Each refused to accept the circumstances of their individual lives as a "reality" for which they had no choice. Every one of us can take a lesson here and refuse to accept circumstance as something that must be a part of our story. And you are capable of doing the same.

Mastermind **Anthony Robbins** reminds us of the importance of awareness and how the roots of most of our problems in life are contained in the *belief* that we are somehow "not good enough." Most of us do not make a conscious decision about what we believe. Rather, our beliefs are based on generalizations we make about our past. Unfortunately, many of us are wired to focus in on the painful experiences of our past and form pessimistic beliefs about what that means for our current state of affairs and the potential for our future.

Most people don't live the life they want,
they live the life they are given.

Dr. Alfred Adler, renowned psychotherapist, recognized the *inferiority complex* as an isolating element that plays a key role in human personality development beginning in early childhood and often continuing throughout adult life. Many people, because of their negative beliefs, *falsely* consider themselves to be limited in some way, shape, or form (intelligence, talent, capability, creativity, or skill). In virtually every case, these beliefs are false narratives we have chosen to adopt as a measure of reality, which affects the perspective of life we develop.

Never forget, you have more potential than you could ever use in your entire lifetime. Think about how profound that statement is. You have competencies and capabilities that have never been tapped. You have the ability, right now, to accomplish virtually any goal you set for yourself...if you are willing to do whatever it takes to achieve it. Make a conscious decision today to change the narrative you have created based on the circumstances of your past. Wake up to the fact that the past does not define you. Remember, you have the power of choice. No one can ever take that from you. Choose wisely.

The Psychology of Winning

Because our beliefs are learned psychological traits, it only goes to reason that what can be learned can also be unlearned. You were born with a clean psychological slate. From that very moment, however, you began the learning process. Each facet of your life— from your influences and academics to your associations, decisions, and experiences—all became a part of the psychological program by which you began writing your life story. You are who you are today based on the entirety of the story you have written to this very moment.

*"May your choices reflect your hopes,
not your fears."*
~ Nelson Mandela

There are many things you believe you *know* about yourself. As true a statement as this is, it also holds true that there is much you do *not* know. The starting point of unlocking more of your true self is for you to become more aware of the world around you. Psychologists call this higher form of self-awareness *Emotional Intelligence* or EI. People with high EI are typically very self-aware. They understand their own emotions and don't allow their feelings to cloud their judgment. Those with a higher self-awareness tend to trust their intuition and do a relatively good job of keeping their emotions in check.

Jack Welch, former CEO of General Electric, described the most important leadership quality as the "reality principle." He defined this as *an ability to see the world as it really is, not as you wish it were.* He would begin almost every meeting to discuss a goal, a strategy, or a problem with the question, "What's the reality?"

If you want to be the best you can be, and to achieve what is truly possible, you must be brutally honest with yourself. You must take the time to analyze yourself from every perspective, in detail, to determine exactly where you are. Your analysis helps you to gain awareness and insight on everything from the conditions to the competition.

Awareness allows us to take an honest look at ourselves from an alternate or outside perspective, which increases our ability to develop emotional intelligence. It also helps us to better recognize and acknowledge our strengths and weaknesses, which allows us to progress toward better performance. Many people believe self-awareness to be the cornerstone of emotional intelligence.

The psychology of winning calls upon us to consider the deeper meaning behind the concept—from one of gamesmanship to one of achievement—through personal enrichment and an appreciation of the present moment. There is so much happening right before our very eyes that we miss altogether when we allow ourselves to be swept away by the insignificance of yesterday or the concerns of tomorrow. Therefore, it is important to strive to catch yourself as your mind is distracted by the thoughts that attempt to steal your attention away from the magnificence of *right now*.

There is a process by which we become better as we get closer to our goals and objectives. This process brings about life changes that increases our awareness and shows us things about ourselves and our surroundings that empower us to think differently. This new way of thinking *awakens* us to things we previously could not see or appreciate.

When you step into awareness, you win! As a winner, you begin adopting a new set of ideals that are empowered by the things you see and appreciate. Your goals become clearer as you are better able to project your objectives and define the steps to get there (goal-setting). Awareness allows you to see most everything, giving you a tactical advantage of overcoming inevitable obstacles through better strategic planning.

Awareness influences your core beliefs, which increases your self-confidence. An increase of self-confidence brings about changes in the way you walk, talk, and act. Because you begin believing you will achieve your goals, you begin to act in a manner that attracts people and opportunities into your life that better enable you to achieve the goals you set for yourself.

Be Your Genuine Self

We humans have a tendency to act "as if." The old-school mentality endorses an often misunderstood "fake it until you make it" mentality whereby the premise is to convince yourself—through acting—that you have already achieved your goal. That's all good until you look around and see that nothing much has changed. Don't get me wrong, there is a subtle connection to the concept of determined practice here, but the old way of thinking has been replaced by a more pragmatic approach that tells us that acting must absolutely be coupled with action.

What this means is that, when you start off, you may not *feel* much like the great success you desire to be. You will not have the self-confidence that comes from a record of successful achievements. You will often doubt your own abilities and have some fear of failure. So, one of the ways to begin re-programming your mind is to act "as if" you have already achieved your goal. Note: This is a beginning methodology that gets your brain *in gear* to bring you into alignment with your goals and objectives.

To act "as if" is a psychological practice. It is not a physical process. So, don't go out and buy a new BMW to support the claim that you're acting "as if" you can afford one. You'll quickly realize that you most likely cannot, and you will end up sabotaging your goal achievement process, not to mention your finances.

When you act "as if" you are already the person you desire to be, with the qualities and talents you desire to have, the actions you take will generate a familiar psychology that you have already begun to program into your mind. You begin behaving consistent with the person you desire to be. You reinforce the development of new, life-enhancing beliefs by increasing your knowledge and skills to a point where you are confident to step up to any demand or challenge. An increase in knowledge is evidenced by confidence, courage, insight, vocabulary, body posture, etc. Your new actions help you to increasingly realize that you are developing, shaping, and controlling the evolution of a new attractive character by the new thoughts, beliefs, and actions you have adopted.

Your growth helps you to accelerate the development of new, positive beliefs by setting bigger and more exciting goals. As a result, you develop new beliefs by taking actions consistent with those beliefs. Your new mindset will better prepare you to take *action* that is congruent with the outcome you seek. Your *new* actions are built upon the new beliefs you have adopted through the successes you are exposed to. Before you know it, you will have grown far more than you ever thought possible.

Remember, your objective is to reprogram your subconscious mind for success and achievement by creating the *psychological equivalent* in everything you do or say. Therefore, it is important to focus on the thoughts and activities that breathe life into your goals.

It is also important to note that you should always be your genuine self, especially while in the programming phase. While it is completely acceptable to seek and follow advice and mentorship, you should never try to be anyone other than yourself. There is a natural tendency to change as we grow personally and progressively make our way to our goals. You should be just fine as long as your personal growth is built upon the genuine core principles that define you.

Write Your Story

It's time to write your story. So, remove the limits of your imagination, cast aside your preconceptions, and give yourself permission to go in any direction you desire. You are the central character. Design a life of your dreams. Where do you live, who are the people in your life, what do you see, smell, hear, and taste? How did you get here? What value do you bring to the world? How do you feel? An amazing thing begins to happen as you write the narrative of your story…you actually begin to believe it. Don't skip this simple but powerful exercise. It can be just what you need to help you go from where you are to where you want to be.

Some Final Thoughts

> **Change your outlook, change your life.** It has been said that a person can light up a room when they walk in or when they walk out. Which type defines you? Do you bring value, enthusiasm, and inspiration to others? Your outlook determines the energy you bring. Even a subtle shift in your outlook can bring profound change to your life. Go ahead, give it a try.

➢ **Seize the moment!** Nothing is accomplished without some kind of action. The natural laws teach us that influence is the catalyst that brings about change. Influence is induced by action. The longer you delay action, the longer you will find yourself right where you are, unable to influence much of anything. Take advantage of the time you have, *right now*, to get started on realizing your goals.

➢ **Things are not always what they seem.** What personal limitations have you accepted that have become part of your story? Are you ready to look past those limitations and re-write the narrative of your life as you intend for it to be instead of what it has become? Never forget, you have more potential than you could ever use in your entire lifetime. You have competencies and capabilities that have never been tapped. You have the ability, right now, to accomplish virtually any goal you set for yourself if you are willing to do whatever it takes to achieve it. Get out of your own way and make something happen!

Thought-provoking questions…

1. What is your story? Is it developing the way you want it to or is it subject to circumstances?

2. How would you rewrite the narrative of your story if you had absolute power to do so? Be specific.

3. What do you see as the limits of your capabilities? What can you do to change that? Do you believe you have the power to change or remove those limitations? What will it take? How long will it take? What resources do you need?

4. It has been said that if you can hold it in your heart, then you can hold it in your hands. It goes to show that, if you can create a goal so compelling that you will do whatever it takes to achieve it, you will indeed possess it. What goal do you have in your heart? Write a short story that speaks to you. Remove the limits of your imagination and show yourself what is possible. The exercise could be quite revealing.

Part Two

∞

GOAL-GETTING

Chapter Eight

Your Fortune

"Fortune favors the prepared mind."
~ Louis Pasteur

The word *fortune* is typically associated with all that is good, as in "good fortune." Fortune is also often associated with luck. "He's fortunate (lucky) to be alive." Anyone reading this book will learn that, in a deliberate and philosophical sense, luck is *where preparation meets opportunity*, especially when taken into the broader context of the goal-achievement process. For the purposes of this chapter, we consider *fortune* as having a positive outcome that can be *controlled* as opposed to the coincidental nature typically associated with luck. A fortune is perceived as being built upon the determined nature of man, whereas luck is seen as an outcome that is subject to the coincidental alignment of good fortune. While both fortune *and* good luck are favorable outcomes when associated with goals, it is easy to see where the lines between the two become blurred. But let's not get ahead of ourselves by getting wrapped up too much in the terminology, because, as we clearly know by now, it's just as good to be lucky as it is to be fortunate. Where the terms tend to collide most is in the perception of others and the effect each has on our personal lives.

The good fortune of a determined mind is quite often perceived as *good luck* by outsiders who know nothing of the amount of determined perseverance and sacrifice of the achiever. Ironically, the critics are among the same people who are quick to declare their own hopes, dreams, and aspirations but fall short of bringing them to life by *acting* on them, all the time wondering why they are not "lucky" like you. They are also the same ones who will ultimately call upon the advice of the achiever to ask about the "secrets" of success. So, be prepared to become a sought-after authority as you progressively achieve your goals.

It's Good to be Fortunate

Good fortune comes to those who prepare themselves for it. Whatever you see as the story of your life is *going* to come true along the lines of your narrative. If you fall short of realizing just how profound that statement is, go back and reread it as many times as it takes to resonate with you. Your life is a reflection of your perception. Your perception is driven by the dominant thoughts and images you have programmed into your mind. If you are not happy with the way your life is working out, you must change the way you see things. Your perception is *so* powerful that even a simple (purposeful) shift can produce extraordinary results.

The power of a positive outlook sounds good on the surface, but the term "positive thinking" has been used so often it is quite easily dismissed as just another cliché. But traditional paradigms are changing. Research is beginning to reveal that a positive outlook can mean much more than a positive attitude. A positive outlook can actually create real value in your life and help you build skills that last much longer than a smile.

There is no doubt that happiness is a result of achievement. But all too often we assume that happiness *always* follows success. It does not. How often have you heard someone say something like, "If I just get that job, I'll be happy," or "If I owned my own restaurant, I'd be happy." There are many people who have achieved undeniable success, and yet, are still not happy. Why? Because happiness is a result of *fulfillment*. Happiness is essential to building the skills that allow for success, but we must be mindful of what we believe will bring us fulfillment. Therefore, happiness should be both a *precursor* to success (driven by perspective) *and* the result of it (fulfillment).

Your good fortune is the result of your outlook, good ideas, and work ethic. This is where the goal-getting process begins. Your personal definition of good fortune is—and should always remain—independent of what other people think. Trust me on this—there will be haters who will not see your success as good fortune. The number one reason for this is because you are no longer like them. The number two reason—they know it! So, stick to your plan to achieve the goals you have set for yourself. Embrace the good fortune that comes your way as a result of your determination to become something bigger than your current self. Seek joy, balance, and insight. Give back from your abundance. Pursue adventure through the many experiences life has to offer. Your brain will do the rest.

Your Fortune is in the Follow-up

Consistency is one of the most overlooked elements of the achievement process. It is paramount—in virtually every aspect—to be consistent. It is not enough to merely set a goal. We must be mindful of the care and feeding of our action plan to reach the goals we set. If we fail to follow through and follow up consistently, we will experience inconsistent results. Inconsistent results produce frustration and uncertainty—two of the most destructive elements to realizing any achievement.

Any initiative, once started, requires consistency in terms of follow-through in order to be effective and to avoid frustration and uncertainty. Think of the salesperson who fails to follow-up with a client or customer. More sales have been lost because of ineffective or non-existent follow-up. Aside from the fact that it just makes good sense in terms of the quality of service, most people (clients, customers, business partners, etc.) require more than one engagement before making a decision.

A friend of mine sells electrical components to major manufacturers. Most of his clients are fully aware that they can find similar quality parts elsewhere in the marketplace—some for even less than they are currently paying. Yet they continue to do business with him. When asked how he has managed to prevent one client from doing business elsewhere for such a long period of time, he responds, with a shrug and a smile, "Because they like me." Do your clients or associates like *you* enough to establish this kind of loyalty?

Part of your job as an effective person of influence is to provide a memorable experience and follow-through with the client to remind them of the features and benefits of your product, service, or proposal. Yes, most customers need to be reminded. So, if you are in business of any kind, your fortune is in the follow-up! When setting a goal (sales, personal, team, etc.), it is just as important.

Imagine setting a personal fitness goal of losing weight, gaining a few pounds of muscle, reducing your run time, or reaching a new milestone in your martial arts studies. What kind of progress would you reasonably expect to make if you are not consistent in your efforts? Your fortune in your fitness objectives *compels* you to follow-through consistently. The difference between champions and spectators is not measured in meters but by fractions. It is the *subtle significance* and the willingness to follow-through consistently that defines the champion.

Is your fortune lost in the lack of follow-up and follow-through? If so, consider the difference a subtle shift would make in your results. Don't over-think this. Just start by making a small, *consistent* effort. Then, watch the changes take place right before your very eyes.

Predict the Future

How many times do you think people attempt to achieve their new goals before they give up? Would it surprise you to learn the average is less than one? How can that be? Because, most people give up before they even get to the action step. Tragic. And the reason they give up is because of all the obstacles, difficulties, problems, and roadblocks that begin to appear...or do they?

Success-minded people take immediate action after they have properly set their goal strategy. They consider the limitations, anticipate the obstacles, and prepare for the setbacks but do not allow any of these elements to get between them and their goal. The fact is, successful people expect setbacks and failures. They see setbacks and failures as learning opportunities. When successful people fail, they know the process. They fall down, learn lessons, pick themselves up, and try again, over and over. They get back on course and follow through to completion. Unsuccessful people try a few things—often referred to as "dabbling"—until they face an obstacle or challenge, quit, and go back to the life they were previously living, which is the life they so desperately wanted to escape in the first place.

While there is value in failure and setbacks, no one actually *enjoys* failing. Fortunately, there are things you can do to reduce the chances of failure and, when it does occur, to get through it as quickly as possible.

First Things First

Identify all the obstacles you can think of that stand between you and your goal before you take any other action. While some obstacles will be obvious (funding, knowledge, processes, etc.), some will not. Write down every single thing you can think of that may potentially present itself as an obstacle to your achievement. Keep in mind that while some things may appear to be obstacles, most obstacles you anticipate never materialize. Next, analyze what you must *do* to either reduce or eliminate all known obstacles. Once again, you will not always be able to predict every eventuality, nor can you expect to have a plan for everything, but by approaching the goal achievement process with an open and aware mind, you are in a much better position to overcome obstacles when they do occur.

Set Your Intentions

Intention is the starting point of every goal. It is your creative power at work as you consider the things that will fulfill your needs and desires. Everything that happens in this world begins with intention. So, if intention is the seed of your hopes, dreams, and aspirations, it only makes sense to conclude that the seed of your intention will never grow if you hold onto it. Therefore, set your intentions onto the fertile ground of your consciousness where they can grow and flourish.

Intent captures the essence of a state of mind. It is a psychological state that represents a commitment to carrying out an act or actions in the future. Intention involves mental activities such as planning and forethought. With this in mind, it is safe to determine that an effective goal achievement plan should be intentional. The power of setting an intentional goal is a significant difference-maker in terms of designing a goal around what you have to give as opposed to what you have to gain. If your intention is to create a goal that brings you prosperity but is not tied, in some manner, to providing value, you may make money, but you are less likely to prosper. Set your intentions with a spirit of giving and you will always prosper.

The most effective method of setting your intention is to find a quiet place and time, preferably during a time you have set aside for prayer, meditation, or deep contemplation, to place the message of your intention into the quiet space between your thoughts. This sacred space is most closely aligned with the still, quiet place of solitude where your innermost self is connected to wisdom, truth, and that which is bigger than your ability to reason or comprehend.

Once you set your intention, let it go. Don't try to hold onto it and labor over the timing or process. Your job of setting it is finished. Allow the results of your intentions to naturally flow to you. Your only responsibility at this point is to follow through on the path of your goal (see *The Fortune is in the Follow-up* section of this chapter). The right intention powers a goal with an underlying assurance that all is well even without evidence of clearly-defined details or timing.

Be Solutions-Minded

Reaching your goals requires you to be *solutions-minded*. Issues and obstacles are inevitable. So, to better handle them, why not begin by describing them in a way that gives *you* power instead of them? Framing the issues as "problems" casts them in a manner that gives *them* power, breathing life into the overwhelming nature of such distractions. Instead, why not refer to obstacles and issues as "projects?" Ah, you can practically *feel* the difference just by using a term that better frames them in a way that brings about solutions instead of headaches.

Solutions-minded people focus their energy on finding a way past obstacles and setbacks as quickly and as efficiently as possible. They rarely give credence to how obstacles affect their progress. They measure progress by their achievements and milestones and learn from the *projects* that initially present themselves as obstacles and setbacks. They don't spend time talking about difficulties, and they never use them as excuses to slow down.

Some people think about obstacles and setbacks as problems and difficulties, spending most of their time talking about how their progress has been slowed by the obstacles. They are quick to leverage their problems into excuses for why their progress is slow or nonexistent. Problem-oriented people talk continuously about their problems, about who or what caused them, how unhappy or angry they are, and how unfortunate it is that they are mired in difficulty, which leads to continued stress, strife, and failure—everything they seek to escape.

Between you and most anything you desire to accomplish will lie a problem or an obstacle of some kind. This is life's way of challenging your resolve to accomplish something worthwhile and is even considered by some as a rite of passage. This is why *success* is sometimes defined as *the slow and steady progress* toward a worthy goal or objective. Achievers have developed an ability to solve the problems that stand between them and their objectives. They do it efficiently and in a determined manner so they can get back to enjoying the journey toward the accomplishment of their goals.

Nothing is New Forever

Fortunately, problem solving is a learned skill. Much like riding a bicycle or mastering a new language, solving issues can also be mastered. Of course, no two issues or problems are the same, and therefore will always require some creativity, analysis, and imagination. But the more you focus on solutions, the better you will become at handling them with confidence.

Fortunately, the more problems you solve, the better you become at solving them. The better you are at solving them, the more proficient you will become as subsequent issues arise. In fact, your ability to handle the small problems better prepares you to handle increasingly bigger issues. Eventually, you will be solving problems that can have significant financial consequences. As new problems arise, you will eventually learn how much less intimidated you are as the novelty of handling problems becomes more familiar to you. Familiarity brings with it a certain level of confidence that is developed by experience. So, don't fear that which is new and unfamiliar. It will not always be so unfamiliar.

You have the ability to solve virtually any problem and to overcome any obstacle that may arise on the path to your goal. In fact, you have within you, right now, all the intelligence and ability you will ever need to overcome any obstacle that could possibly keep you from reaching your goals. All you have to do is summon the determination that already resides within and allow it to help you discover the answers that already exist.

The Compression Factor

Between you and most anything you want to accomplish, there are obstacles or limiting factors that determine the speed at which you get from where you are to where you want to go.

For example, if you are flying in to a major airport hub (Atlanta, Chicago, Los Angeles) you will inevitably encounter a delay due to air traffic congestion or inclement weather that is narrowing all the traffic into the airport. Air traffic controllers refer to this narrowing as "compression." The compression becomes a part of the equation that factors into whether or not you make an on-time arrival and can make it to your connecting flights. The speed at which you are able to pass through the compression point will largely affect the speed of your entire journey. Eliminate the narrowing and you eliminate or reduce the compression. Reducing or eliminating the compression *increases* the flow (efficiency or speed) of accomplishment.

In accomplishing any major goal, there is always a constraint or chokepoint you must get through. Your objective is to accurately identify it and then focus all of your energies on making your way through the compression as efficiently as possible. Speed is important. But it is not as important as an accurate analysis on where you are, how you got there, and your plan to get beyond the delay. Your ability to carefully and accurately remove or reduce the compression will help you move ahead faster and *then* focus on speed. In this case, *slowing down* (to analyze, assess, and act) will actually help you to get to your objective faster.

This is not the time to make rash decisions or turn around and run. It is not the time to over-analyze or become overwhelmed by the high volume of traffic in front of you. It is a time for patience as you consider the reasons you created the goal in the first place. Recognize the situation for what it is—a time for careful self-deliberation, analysis, education, and action. Tap into your *why* and find the determination required to keep going. Then, when you break out of the compression—and you will break out—you will have persevered through a process from which most others have retreated. You will emerge a completely changed person if you keep moving toward your goal, even if it's one carefully calculated step after another. This process alone has been one of the most effective among today's millionaires. Follow it, and you, too, will experience your own personal breakthrough beyond anything you have ever experienced.

"When you're going through hell, keep going."
~ Winston Churchill

Fear and Doubt

The two major obstacles to success and achievement are *fear* and *doubt*. Fear limits an average person in thought and deed (action). The mere thought of doing something extraordinary can be paralyzing to some people, keeping them from even *considering* taking action to break through the ruse fear creates. This is one reason why the average number of times a person attempts a new goal is less than one. The grip of fear can be so powerful it can alter the very course of our lives if we allow it.

The second obstacle—closely aligned to fear—is self-doubt. This obstacle stems from a comparison we make of ourselves to everyone else, and how we begin to think everyone else is somehow better, smarter, and far superior than we are. The problem with this perspective—aside from it being the worst possible measure of self-worth—is that we compare our *weaknesses* to the *strengths* of others. So, essentially, we lose from the start. You are unique in that no one else on the planet has or will ever have your personal genetic makeup. Your ideas and inspirations are a product of who you are as an individual, and no can or ever will be able to reproduce that.

The Process of *Un*learning

If there is anything good about fear and doubt it is that they are both *learned* emotions. Whatever has been learned can, fortunately, be *unlearned*, through practice, repetition, and determination.

The remedies to doubt and fear are *courage* and *confidence*. Higher levels of courage and confidence mean lower levels of fear and doubt—and the less effect these negative emotions have on our performance and behavior.

The way to best develop courage and confidence is with knowledge and preparation. Most fears and doubts stem from ignorance and feelings of inadequacy of some kind. In short, we recognize a deficiency and realize that, without the necessary skillset, we are bound to fail at the very least, and could in fact injure ourselves in the process, causing our worst-case imaginations to go into overdrive.

The more knowledge we gain about our goal or objective, the less fear and anxiety we will encounter, and the more courage and confidence we will have. Think about how you felt before mastering a skill, say, riding a bicycle for the first time. If you're like most, your determination for learning this new skill was enough to help you overcome the presence of fear, but you still needed to develop the skills to accomplish your goal. With the assistance of consistent practice and determination, you were eventually able to master the knowledge and skills of riding a bicycle, and as your skills increased, so, too, did your confidence.

Today, you can quite comfortably look back upon your learning experience as one in which you overcame the element of fear to accomplish your goal. Chances are there are few, if any, remnants of fear remaining with this specific goal. You became so competent at riding a bicycle that you can now do it without even thinking about it. The same principles apply to the skills you need to learn to achieve any goal you set for yourself. Want to learn a new language? Apply the same principles and, before you know it, you'll add another language skillset to your repertoire.

Describe Your Obstacles as Goals

Most obstacles can be easily overcome once they are accurately identified. Some, however, require a bit more planning, effort, and determination to overcome so you can get back on the path to success and achievement. Once you discover a major obstacle, consider making it part of your goal planning strategy by labeling *it* as a goal. If, for example, your major obstacle is a deficiency in knowledge, you could map it as a goal to obtain the requisite knowhow to continue pursuing your goal. In doing so, be sure to be as specific as possible in identifying both the obstacle *and* the goal.

General concept

OBSTACLE: Temporary lack of knowledge

GOAL: Upgrade my skills and abilities to learn what I need to know to continue progressing toward my goals

METHOD: Enroll and pass a specific course of instruction

Specific concept

OBSTACLE: Lack of knowledge on how to acquire the financial resources to invest in rental property

GOAL: Find and hire a mentor. Purchase my first income-producing rental property in the local area by (specific date), by following the philosophies and principles of my mentor

METHOD: Work 20 hours a week part-time to raise the capital and invest the proceeds into a stock or mutual fund until the funding goal is met. Then, use the knowledge I have gained to leverage my money and probability of success

As you can see from the above examples, there are two ways to "convert" your obstacle into a goal. The two methods are provided to re-emphasize and remind you of the importance of being as specific as possible, just as you would be when mapping out your primary goals.

So, using the situations above as examples, consider making a list of all the things that you could *do* to increase your knowledge and skills, improve your time management, and access resources to increase your efficiency and effectiveness. Set deadlines and post measures next to each step in your goal-mapping strategy in order to achieve your objectives. Then select *one* key task and take action on it immediately. Become accountable to yourself as you continue making steady progress toward your goals.

If you have any questions or concerns about the accuracy of your obstacle, discuss it with someone you know and trust to give you an objective assessment of their perspective. Get out of your own way by putting your ego aside. Invite and respond to honest feedback and criticism. Be open to the possibility that you have fundamental flaws and weaknesses that are standing in the way of you realizing your full potential. Once your obstacle is clear to you, ideas, opportunities, and answers will begin to come to you.

Respond to every one of these as if you have personally called upon each one, because, in essence, that is *exactly* what you have done. As you respond, you will begin to attract all kinds of helpful resources that will enable you to overcome the obstacles that will better enable you to move rapidly and efficiently toward your goals.

For every problem or obstacle that is standing between you and what you want, there is a solution. Your job is to be absolutely clear about what limits the speed at which you achieve your goal and then to focus your time, effort, and attention on alleviating or eliminating that limitation. By removing your major obstacles, you will often make more progress in a just a few months than the average person makes in several years.

Some Final Thoughts

The fate of your fortune is in your hands. If that sounds like a huge responsibility, it is. But instead of being intimidated at the thought of that responsibility, take ownership and get to work. Remember, it's good to be fortunate. With a few simple steps, you can be well on your way to shaping your own fortune inside the goal-setting process.

> ➢ **Your Fortune is in the Follow-up.** Consistency is the watchword here. Follow through and follow up are key aspects of creating and sustaining momentum vital to the health of your goal-achievement process.

> ➢ **Predict the Future.** Identify all the obstacles you can think of that stand between you and your goal before you take any other action. Write down every single thing you can think of that may potentially present itself as an obstacle to your achievement. Next, analyze what you must *do* to either reduce or eliminate all known obstacles.

➤ **Set Your Intentions.** Recall the elements to helping you accurately predict the future in terms of knowing that you will achieve your goals. Set your intentions to reach your goals, no matter what, and be solutions-minded. Claim power and dominion over your goals from the start. You are the creator of your goals; therefore, *you* have the most power, not your circumstances.

➤ **Nothing is New Forever.** As you are faced with new concepts and challenges, remember that nothing is new forever. As you look past the surface of a new concept, issue, or obstacle, seek to discover ways in which to overcome them and learn from them. No one is expected to know everything. Therefore, you may have to take the time to learn new concepts, methods, and tactics to eliminate the inevitable chokepoints that arise from time to time.

Thought-provoking questions…

1. What comes to mind when you think of being fortunate? Are you embracing your fortune or resisting it?

2. Are you absolutely convinced that you *deserve* to reach your goals? That should be a relatively easy answer…unless you know with certainty that you're *not* doing whatever it takes to ensure the successful outcome of your fortune. Is your outlook aligned with your intentions? In other words, are you just *interested* in the successful outcome of your goals, or are you *committed* to them? The differences are subtle, but the outcome is significant.

3. Are you psychologically prepared to take on the challenges of learning something new in order to have the knowledge that most others don't have so you can achieve what most

others will not? The manner in which you take on new learning objectives is critical to the successful outcome of your fortune.

Chapter Nine

The Most Important Part of the Goal

*"It takes courage to grow up and
become who you really are."*
~ E.E. Cummings

One of the most compelling characteristics of successful achievers is that they know who they are, what they believe in, and what they stand for. At the very core of our individual personalities lies our values. Human values are the *virtues* that guide us to take the actions we do as we interact with others and pursue our dreams, goals, and aspirations. Our values define us and create the platform upon which we operate the premise of our lives.

Our external actions are largely controlled by the things we value, that is, the *beliefs* we have about ourselves and the world around us. Our beliefs are largely determined by the *perspectives* we have of the world and the fundamental morality we embrace to measure the standard of our lives. Although it may not seem like it, our values are constantly changing. To believe otherwise is an admission that *we*, as a people, are not changing. Nothing could be further from the truth because, as we have already learned, the only true constant in life is change itself.

When it comes to goals, the one element that sets the dividing line between achievers and non-achievers is *conviction*. Conviction is driven by our values, which are supported by our motives, which are driven by our beliefs, the combination of which produce the results that are powered by our *actions*. Hopefully you're beginning to discover a pattern.

Some people overcomplicate the goal-achieving process when, in reality, it is fairly simple to master. For these people, achievement is believed to occur "naturally" somehow, as if by fate or accident. They do not believe the achievement process is connected to the power of human values and to the compelling nature of action. This kind of thinking could not be further from the truth.

YOU are at the Center of it all

Regardless of what you are told, the "secrets" you discover, or the formulas you may possess, *nothing* will work if you are not willing to do *whatever it takes* to reach your goals. *You* are at the center of the entire goal achievement process. If your goal is not coming fast enough then *you* must do something different to accelerate it. If *you* are met by frustration, then it is *you* who must conduct a self-analysis to determine what *you* need to do for things to change.

> *"For life to change, you must change."*
> ~ Jim Rohn

Change can cause a great deal of stress for people who have rigid belief systems. Those people tend to be very comfortable with what they are doing—their current methods and processes for handling things—and are typically unwilling to change, even in the face of overwhelming evidence to the contrary. Don't let this be you.

The real questions you should be asking are: *Does what I'm doing work? Are my methods achieving results? Are my actions the best actions to support my goals?* The only thing that matters is whether a particular decision or course of action is effective in accomplishing the results of the goals you have set.

So, if *you* are indeed at the center of it all, then perhaps a review of your personal inclinations is in order. I have found that most people don't need to be *educated* as much as they need to be *reminded,* so a review is typically all that is needed to remind us of the power we truly possess to affect change. As some of this information may present itself as educational, some of it will no doubt strike a familiar chord as well. However, just because we may *know* something does not always translate to the fact that we are actually *applying* what we know.

Consider the Self-Identity diagram below. Each concentric ring identifies a psychological or emotional element that is a part of an overall personality trait, which contributes to and builds upon the overall makeup of who we are as individuals. This diagram and the elements go a long way toward explaining why we do the things we do, which can help determine why some of us achieve things easily while others do not.

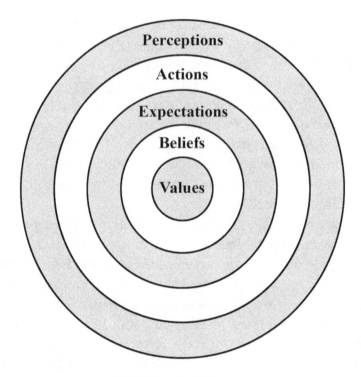

Self-Identity Diagram

Values

Living in alignment with our true **values** leads to self-confidence, self-respect, and personal pride. A greater sense of clarity develops the closer we operate to our core values. A close examination of our values goes a long way to help determine what we truly want from life. The degree of *value* we associate with the outcomes influences our behavior (commitment, consistency, follow-through, etc.) to any given task or endeavor. For example, we assign value to a goal we set according to the relative importance and impact it may have upon our life. The value(s) we assign fluctuates according to several factors—chief among them are individual and cultural standards along with an assessment and analysis of effort versus outcome.

Low value typically equates to a reluctance to expend or invest any great amount of effort on a task of relative *unimportance*. So how do we know what our true values are, and how can we better align ourselves with them for a more favorable outcome?

We always demonstrate our true values by our *actions*—most especially our actions *under pressure*. Whenever we are forced to choose between one behavior and another, we will always act consistent with what is most important and valuable to us at any given moment.

One of the most revealing exercises you can conduct to determine *who* you really are, and *what* you really want, is to prioritize your values. Once you are clear about the relative importance of your values, you can then organize your outer life so that it is in alignment with your values—or your inner life.

Imagine your personality as concentric rings around an epicenter that encircles your values. Everything feeds your values, which in turn, has an effect upon the actions you take (or refrain from taking) in life. Having already covered the core of your personality—your values—let us examine each of the elements of your personality that supports the epicenter of what makes you…you.

Beliefs

One of the strongest influences on our core values comes from our self-beliefs. Our **beliefs** govern the strategies we employ and the rituals we keep as we set out to accomplish a goal or objective and, as stated earlier, define the self-imposed limitations we place upon ourselves as we determine just how far we will go to achieve a goal. If you desire to achieve something far greater than you ever have, it may be time to re-evaluate your beliefs to determine whether you currently have what it takes to pursue your new goal. If not, don't sweat it. Just examine your beliefs and make the necessary adjustments to pursue an appropriate goal that's better suited to align with your core beliefs.

The forces that drive and direct our behavior are based on a series of implicit beliefs we have about ourselves. Collectively, these self-beliefs determine the direction and intensity of our motivation and action in virtually every area of our lives. Beliefs help us determine what we will do, how we do it, and how we judge our own accomplishments in relation to the rest of the world. These very same beliefs also have a limitation attached to them that we assign based solely upon how we formed them in the first place.

Our beliefs are so intimately connected to our values that they are largely responsible for the career choices we make, the relationships we seek, and ultimately, what we do or do not accomplish in life. Self-beliefs form the guiding principles we have created about our personal capabilities. They help us determine what is or is not successful in terms of outcomes that we expect from any given situation or life circumstance. Bringing our beliefs to the forefront of conscious awareness helps us to take the steps that harness the power and influence of those beliefs. So, what are some of the aspects of our beliefs we should strive to be more aware of?

Control – The most dominant self-belief we have is the degree of control we think we have over our own destiny. Those with an external focus believe their destiny is not within their direct control, whereas those with strong control beliefs feel more in command of their ability to influence and shape outcomes. This internal focus influences personal growth and development because it drives a person to take responsibility and accountability for their own success, setbacks, or outright failures.

Competence – Some people tend to appraise their degree of competency not on actual ability or knowledge but upon *presumed* competency beliefs, including the *perception* of their competence held by others. Competence assessments can influence perceptions of overall self-worth and can oftentimes be the deciding factor in determining whether we engage in a task, elect to defer, or withdraw completely to avoid a challenge. Avoidance is almost always motivated by fear of some kind and can typically be overcome by education, counseling, or clinical intervention.

Expectations

Our beliefs determine and affect the third ring of our personality—our **expectations**. If we believe we have positive values, we tend to believe that we are a "good" person. If we believe we are good, then we also believe that good things will happen to us. Our belief or outlook has a lot to do with how we feel. Therefore, it is only logical for us to feel positive or cheerful in what we expect will happen for us.

"Good things come to those who wait."
~ Violet Fane

Our attitude is an outward reflection of our values that is shaped by our expectations. For example, if you believe the world is generally a place of goodness and that you will be very successful in life, your expectations will begin to take shape around that narrative. You will begin to expect that most everything that happens to you is helping you in some way, shape, or form. This is why a positive mental attitude is an absolute essential element in the formula of success.

The more we believe, the more we expect. Expectation, in this example, is *not* a negative trait. Expectation, based on a sincere attitude of goodness, opens the eyes of the seeker and exposes a person to opportunity. *Expectation* is an attitude that opens the pathways for goodness to thrive and for opportunity to reveal itself. Your expectation influences you to look for the good in others and in most all situations. This perspective reveals things to those with a "fresh set of eyes" and places them in a prime position for seizing opportunity as soon as it presents itself...which brings us to the next level of our personality—*Action!*

Actions

Our **actions** are a direct reflection of our innermost values. Our achievements are driven more by what is going on *inside* of us than by any other factor. It is one of the reasons a positive-minded, goal-oriented person tends to live a happier and successful, prosperous life—largely because of the internal programming that drives them.

It has been said that man is happiest when his internal programming is congruent with his external actions. When we are living in complete alignment with our values, we are operating at our happiest, most positive state. This positive state empowers us and paves the way for bold, convicted decision-making the likes of which bring about results and the successful accomplishment of goals.

If our goals and values are not in alignment, we are more likely to be met by frustration and disappointment as we struggle to figure out the reasons why. Our crystal-clear understanding of our values leads us to an unmistakable commitment to achievement that is bolstered by what we believe to be of absolute importance in life. It is understanding and a connection to our values that forms the basis by which we can begin to construct and organize our goals in alignment with our beliefs and values.

Perceptions

A still, small voice of reason and insight speaks to us in a manner that shapes the **perceptions** of our life. The narrative is influenced by the culmination of experiences we have had over the course of our lives right up to this very moment. If we are in touch with the quiet leading of our inner voice of reason, we are said to be perceptive, or aware. Awareness helps us to gain clarity on the broader aspect of life, revealing an interconnectedness with…everything.

Awareness helps us to sharpen our perceptive senses and aligns us with our true values, effectively completing the circle of self-identity and true introspection. Wisdom is said to be intimately connected to a higher level of perception, which is broadly believed to be connected to a power greater than our self. When we experience wisdom, our sense of self-trust increases dramatically, leading to a greater sense of intuition. It is this sense of self-trust that contains the power to greatness.

What Do You Really Want?

There are a number of insightful ways to help you to determine what you truly want from life. First, you should consider all the aspects of the self-identity diagram, taking particular note of how each of the elements affects the core of who you are—your values.

How have you acted under pressure in the past? How did you react when presented with choices that conflicted with your values, beliefs, and expectations? Although the past does not entirely describe who you are today, it does provide insight that will give you an indication of your predominant values at that time.

What makes you feel important? What raises your self-esteem? What increases your sense of self-respect and personal pride? What have you accomplished in your past that has given you a great sense of pride and satisfaction? The answers to these questions, and others like them, will help identify your values, beliefs, and expectations, which will go a long way to help determine what you want out of life.

"Tell me what gives a person his greatest feeling of importance, and I will tell you his entire philosophy of life."
~ Dale Carnegie

What is it that you desire more than anything else? What is it that, deep down in your heart, more than anything else, you have a burning desire to be, have, do, or become in life? What do you want to be known for?

What words would you like people to use to describe you? What would you like people to say about you when you have passed on? How do you want your family, friends, and children to remember you? What *legacy* would you like to leave behind?

What kind of reputation do you have today? What kind of reputation would you like to develop? What would you have to begin doing *today* in order to create the kind of reputation you desire?

Knowing *who* you are is essential in defining *what* you want— your dreams, hopes, goals, and aspirations. Clarity of purpose is connected to an ability to clearly define your goals and objectives. Connect these two aspects, and you are well on your way to achievement.

The Past

If given a choice, many of us would welcome an opportunity to revisit the past to correct some of the choices we made that have become an unwanted part of who we are today. While some of us have had difficult experiences throughout life, some have simply made choices that were not the best we *could* have made. Many of us continue to make some of the very same ill-advised decisions today, only to live with the consequences of regret, dissatisfaction, and discontent. Some of you have fallen onto hard times and have begun to lose hope of ever finding a way out of your current circumstances. Rest assured, there is *always* a way out.

Your past holds no value beyond the lessons it provides in terms of how it has shaped your current values and beliefs. That's not to say it is irrelevant to the present or the future, but your past is just that—the past. Dwelling on your past mistakes can lure you into a state of regret. Instead of focusing on all the mistakes and missteps you've made (we've all made them), focus on the lesson those missteps have taught you. Then, do something to adjust your path using the lessons you have learned. If you do nothing, you are apt to repeat history and reignite regret. Consider the candid reflection of the woman in the following short story.

As my friend rested in her hospital bed this evening, desperately fighting pancreatic cancer, she squeezed my hand tight and said, "Promise me, no matter how good or bad you have it, you will wake up every morning thankful for your life. Because every morning you wake up, someone somewhere will be desperately fighting for theirs."

Sooner or later, we all *decide* to change. The real question is whether we want to change bad enough to actually *do* something about it. Because, as we know all too well by now, a decision to change is just a decision until we take *action*. Decisions, backed by actions and a burning desire for change, produce results. It is a universal law of cause and effect.

Get to Know Your (Inner) Self

Psychologists tell us our self-esteem determines our level of happiness. Self-esteem is defined as: *Confidence in one's own worth or abilities.* In other words, your self-esteem is determined by the confidence you have in yourself—that is, how you see yourself as judged by the standards and ideals *you* set for yourself. Your ideals are created by the values, goals, hopes, dreams, and aspirations you have for yourself. Psychologists also tell us that the more our behavior is consistent with what we feel our *ideal* behavior should be, the more likely we are to respect ourselves, and thus, the happier we tend to be. Conversely, whenever we behave in a manner that is inconsistent with our ideals, the more likely we will be to experience a negative self-image or, at the very least, feel off-balance or out of alignment. So, what is a good way to ensure our behavior is more consistent with our ideals?

Aligning our behaviors to the standards and ideals we set for ourselves drives a need for greater awareness through self-analysis. One often-used method of self-analysis is to look within yourself to identify the elements (in your personality, temperament, skills, abilities, habits, education, or experience) that could be holding you back from achieving the goals you have set.

The 80/20 Rule applies to the limitations that exist between you and your goals. This rule says that 80% of your limitations are internal, while 20% of your limitations are external influences—other people and "outside" situations. In other words, the majority of your limitations are self-imposed. So, if you're ready to accelerate your progress to achievement, be willing to ask the tough questions of yourself for the insight and awareness you need to overcome your internal limitations. "What is it about me that's holding me back?" "What do I need to do to overcome my own self-imposed limitations?" The moment you begin walking, talking, and behaving in ways that are consistent with your highest ideals, your self-image improves, your self-esteem increases, and you feel happier about yourself and the world around you. You feel connected, balanced, valuable, successful, and happy.

The best prescription for a healthy self-esteem is to strive daily to deliberately, systematically, and consistently seek out ways to create circumstances that feed your self-confidence in *everything* you do. Start living your life as if you were already the outstanding person you intend to become, and the outstanding person will emerge. Don't wait. Adopt this fresh new attitude immediately!

What Do You Believe?

Your values play a critical role in determining your beliefs. Your beliefs shape your identity, and thus reveal quite a bit about your true feelings. Your beliefs determine your predisposition for the pursuit of…everything. If your beliefs conflict with any aspect of a goal or objective, you will likely fall short of achieving it, if in fact you elect to pursue it at all. Beliefs determine the level of your conviction and commitment. So, if you are to pursue a goal, you must first consider the role your belief system plays and whether you need to change the underlying beliefs you have *before* you set out on the path to pursue your goals. The alternative is to simply choose a different goal—one that is better aligned with your belief system.

It is surprisingly easy to achieve a goal and still not be happy with who you are as a person. There are plenty of unhappy achievers in this world. While there is certainly nothing wrong with achievement, it is very easy to forget to ask yourself the more important questions that help assure a successful outcome: *Who am I? What do I believe about (myself, this goal, the circumstances it will create, etc.)? How will my identity change as a result of achieving this goal?*

One way to avoid the inevitable head-on collision with a worthy goal is to match your values and beliefs with the projected outcome you expect for your life once you achieve your goal. If the goal is in line with your values, you'll know it. You'll be empowered, encouraged, and happy. If not, you'll also know it.

Don't waste your life on work you don't enjoy. It may or may not be obvious to you, but spending time on anything you don't enjoy will make you miserable. If your goal is tied to joy, there will always be success. If it is tied to money, there *may* be some joy, but never true fulfillment. Do what you love, and what you love will pay you back in overwhelming avalanches of abundance in more ways than you can imagine.

The Right Frame of Mind

You become what you think. What you think, and the manner in which you frame it, influences your beliefs. Your beliefs, as we have discussed, shape your reality. The more you live your life consistent with your beliefs, the happier, healthier, more positive, and energetic your reality will be.

One of the most sacred values is that of *integrity*. Integrity is often one of the most misunderstood terms. At its core, integrity combines a set of personal ideals that embodies consistency, honesty, and accuracy. Consistency calls upon your ability to produce the same effort regardless of the situation. It is a choice you make as a leader, day-in and day-out, even when less than ideal conditions exist. Honesty and accuracy speak to your *intentions* of sincerity, authenticity, and personal pride to complete a task to the utmost of your abilities, and when you are unable, to seek the assistance and advice of others.

Your level of integrity aligns you with a personal code of ethics that is directly tied to your core values. Your core values drive your determination to follow through on your commitment and remain focused on your goals. The higher your level of integrity, the more driven you will be in everything you do. The more driven you are, the faster your results will appear.

Some Final Thoughts

> ➤ **YOU are always in control.** I typically get into the most spirited debates on this point. Most people are quick to point out how the statement implies that we control everything that happens around us. That perspective could not be further from the truth. While we certainly cannot control every circumstance, we *can* control how we *respond* to the things that happen to us or around us. While it is true that we may lose a job, suffer an injury or illness, or find ourselves in "unfortunate" circumstances, we will always have the one thing no one will ever be able to take from us—the power of choice. How you choose to handle things makes all the difference in the second- and third-order effects. Choose well.

➤ **Know yourself.** A clear and intimate connection with our core values is an essential aspect to the goal attainment process. Knowing our self—our beliefs, expectations, actions, and perceptions—provides an unmistakable assurance that the goals we set are the *right* goals. The *right* goals are simply defined as those that are aligned with the tenets of our values. Pursuing the right goals for the right reasons is the best formula for success. That is not to say there won't be challenges, but the best way to overcome challenges is for the goal to be in alignment with our core values. Your values support your deep-seeded convictions—those *internal* elements that drive your *external* actions, which help you form the strategies and solutions needed to overcome challenges to reach your goals.

➤ **Determine what you want.** Ask most people if they want a million dollars and you'll get a resounding "yes!" However, a deeper look into the diversity of the answer will reveal that while most people would certainly like to *have* a million dollars, the majority want to *spend* a million dollars. The difference between the spenders, the savers, and the investors are separated by the values (*beliefs, expectations, perceptions, and most certainly, the actions*) they possess. A clear determination of a desired outcome is an important part of the goal-setting process. Our values help us clarify the goals we set. Clarity is critical. Without it, we have no way of knowing whether the goal is right, nor do we know whether we are moving toward or away from our goal. Define every goal with clarity and connect it with your values, and you will be well on your way to achievement.

Thought-provoking questions...

1. Make a list of the terms that immediately come to mind while thinking of your values. How can you connect these traits with the virtues you have that will help you reach your goals?

2. What actions (habits, rituals, etc.) do you need to change that will enhance your ability to meet or exceed your goals? How would your habits and rituals change if you were living consistent with your values?

3. What is your personal outlook on life? Is it generally positive, negative, cynical, or indifferent? Use this baseline as a starting point to begin understanding yourself better and respond to the changes that you know you must make.

Chapter Ten

Self-Worth

"Everything that happens to you is a reflection of what you believe about yourself."
~ *Iyanla Vanzant*

The absolute best way to ensure you *never* fully realize your hopes, dreams, goals, and aspirations is to beat yourself up over the things you have yet to master or achieve. One of the vulnerabilities of the goal achievement process is the potential to become so focused on your plan of achievement that you begin unknowingly connecting achievement to self-worth. Self-worth should *never* be connected to achievement. That's right, just because you may have climbed to the top echelons of your field in whatever it is you do, does not—and *should* not—define the essence of who you are. Because just as surely as you allow your achievements to define you, you will inevitably experience a setback or outright failure of some kind. Then what? The better method of course, is to first establish your greatest sense of self-worth before you ever embark upon the journey of goal-setting and personal achievement. The realistic alternative is to build your self-worth *while* you pursue your goals.

How do you measure *your* self-worth? I'm sure that when you feel good (or not-so-good) about yourself you know it. But how do you *measure* that? We tend to measure our self-worth in a number of ways, mostly by external influences that do not always provide a complete and accurate assessment of self-worth. Some people measure self-worth by the people they associate with, their career, net worth, achievements, their own physical appearance, or any combination of these. The problem with this method is that these indicators are poor measures of self-worth because they are a reflection of *external* sources.

The establishment of your self-worth should ideally begin with a synchronous alignment of your body, mind, and spirit. The delicate balance and alignment of these three aspects support inner peace, harmony, and balance. Don't be so quick to ignore this philosophy if it sounds a bit cosmic or foreign to you. Because, if any one or more of these vital aspects is out of alignment or deficient, you are operating at a disadvantage to an optimum state of balance and will have a difficult time finding real and lasting happiness. For a deeper look into this philosophy, check out my book, *333 – The Power of Equilibrium,* available on Amazon, Barnes & Noble, and other media outlets.

The way you choose to measure your self-worth will serve as a major factor in the choices you make as well as the thoughts that predominate your logic and govern your emotions, and thus, will affect the way you feel about yourself. When you know and accept who you are, and you are generally pleased with the person you have become, you will begin living by a sense of inner peace, even throughout the inevitable highs and lows of life. You will begin to establish an unwavering sense of confidence that is supported by a belief in yourself regardless of circumstances.

So, what role does self-worth play in the goal-achievement process? It happens to be one of the most *crucial* roles of the entire process. You see, by design (the human design), you will manifest no more in life than the level at which you place your self-worth.

> ### *Sometimes the relationship you need to rescue is the one you have with yourself.*

Self-worth is *the* key to living a happy life. When we don't feel good about ourselves, we're not able to function at our peak state. A less-than-optimal state keeps us from appreciating all the great things life has to offer, which keeps us from imagining the possibility of anything more in terms of developing goals that lead to the greater version of ourselves.

If you are constantly trying to change who you are in order to feel better, it simply will not work. There is nothing wrong with change, mind you. But if you're looking to change as a means to escape who you truly are, then you're going about it all wrong. There is a better way.

You Are Enough

One of the biggest mistakes we *all* make at one time or another is to look outside ourselves for the validation of our self-worth. We seek the approval of others or look for ways to prove our self-worth by the compliments we receive, the things we collect, or the amount of money we earn. The problem with this method is that it will ultimately disappoint you. The reason it will disappoint you is because self-worth can *never* be truly measured by *external* influences.

To gain a real sense of your self-worth, you must access it from the inside-out. How you feel about yourself (inward) at any given point is manifested by your (outward) behavior and attitudes. Your external behavior—from how you treat others to the intentions and expectations you have—are all driven by your internal processes, which are governed at its core on the basis of your self-worth. This is a crucial aspect of the goal mind process of which you should be keenly aware.

You are vulnerable. Okay, so with that uncomfortable statement out of the way, allow me to explain how your vulnerability is a *strength* and not a weakness, as it is typically perceived by the masses. We typically see vulnerability as emotional risk, exposure, and uncertainty, but it is our most accurate measure of courage. Therefore, I *encourage* you to embrace your vulnerabilities rather than avoid them.

"Vulnerability is the birthplace of innovation, creativity, and change."
~ Brené Brown

There is no goal you can achieve that will convince you that you are enough. To realize your greatest achievements—those things that still await you and the experiences you desire—you *must* acknowledge your vulnerabilities.

Perspective check—no one is better or smarter than you. People are just better or smarter in different areas than you. The people who are doing better in some area of business or personal achievement have learned the essential skills to a degree that may currently seem further along than you. If you are not achieving what others are achieving, it simply means that you have not learned what they have learned…yet. Rest assured, you can achieve whatever they achieved if it is your will to do so *and* it aligns with who you are.

Your adaptability to change requires a level of vulnerability. It is your vulnerabilities that will lead you to some extraordinary places…if you allow them to. Your vulnerability tells you that you don't know it all, but you *can* know *enough* to do, be, have, or become anything you want.

Perfection

Perfection exists only in the mind or eyes of the beholder. Even so, things are never truly *perfect* for very long. To strive for perfection is unrealistic. You will never be perfect, but you will *always* be enough. Once you develop that belief, no one and nothing can ever take that from you. Circumstances will change, friendships will fade, and possessions will depreciate, but the level of your self-worth will continue to hold its value and could, in fact, *increase* in value with the right awareness and mindset. So, embrace who you are, cultivate the gifts you possess, and acknowledge the value you truly have.

We very often short-change ourselves using the yardstick of perfection. How many times have you said to yourself, "I'm going to start my plan of action just as soon as I'm ready and things (including you) are perfect"? As attractive as that may seem, it will never happen…because perfection never happens.

Perfectionism is not about striving for excellence. Rather, it is a way of thinking and feeling that says, "If I look perfect, do it perfect, and live perfect, I can avoid or mitigate shame, blame, and judgment." Perfectionism is the ultimate fear of those who are afraid the world is going to see them for who they really are, and they will somehow not measure up. Stop striving for something that does not truly exist, and you will release the things that limit you from becoming all you are meant to become.

Failure is Inevitable

So, now that you realize how vulnerable you are and that you will never be perfect, I have some more "good" news for you. A great many of your endeavors for achievement and goal attainment will likely fail…at least a few times, if not several, before you succeed. While I will never be one who tells you to embrace failure, I *will* tell you that those who *acknowledge* failure see it for the inherent value it truly has. Failure brings about lessons on insight and comprehension that will invariably propel you forward beyond your wildest imagination, and most certainly beyond those who are paralyzed by the thought of doing something different to bring about the changes *they* desire.

Failure is most closely associated with all the things we fear. Fear is known to be the number one obstacle to our successes. Fear prevents or significantly affects the decisions we make. Yet, despite knowing this, we often allow fear to control the actions we take (or refrain from taking) in the process of striving to reach our goals. Giving in to fear can lead to stagnation and ultimately, failure in its purest form. And that should *never* be an option.

There's absolutely nothing wrong with failure...as long as it's recognized for what it is and what it isn't. Allow it to become an obstacle to your dreams and desires, and it takes on a life of limitation, doubt, and insufficiency. Put in its place, however, failure can serve as a useful educational tool that helps us to better evaluate the obstacles or hurdles we must overcome to achieve our goals, objectives, and desires. Failure also provides value in terms of the lessons it provides on what *not* to do.

A State of Mind

Give yourself the life you really want even *before* you have it. To better explain this leading statement, we should first *define* the life we really want. In order to do that, we must consider *why* we want it as well as the influences that affect our desire to obtain it. As you have seen throughout the chapters of this book, your *why* is at the epicenter of what drives you and is a critical factor in the state of mind you adopt in the creation of the kind of life you desire. For a recap on the perspective of our why and the effect its *influence* has on our psychological mindset, return to Chapter Three.

Greatness begins in the mind and heart of the achiever. As you know by now, the power of personal belief is strong. Once we formulate a goal that is crafted by a crystal-clear image or vision, we have the ability to achieve it. Coupling this with a direct link to the center of our why creates a compelling drive that is far superior to a wish or simple desire.

Keep in mind that success does not have to be a lengthy journey. It really does come down to a state of mind you develop and ultimately embrace when your goals are aligned with your ideals. Know this…success lies outside of the material trappings of life. Don't get me wrong, I enjoy having the freedoms that money can buy…*if* it indeed buys freedom and does not keep you tethered to discontent, stress, expectations, and misery. The essence of success is happiness, satisfaction, and contentment with yourself and the world around you. How do *you* honestly define success? Make it a point of your life to develop the right state of mind with respect to how you view success, and I promise you'll find happiness and fulfillment along the way as well.

The Company You Keep

Like it or not, you are a product of the company you keep. When it comes to relationships, we are greatly influenced by those closest to us. People affect our way of thinking, our self-esteem, and our decisions. Of course, we are all individuals, but research has shown that we are highly influenced by our environment and the people we most closely associate with. Bottom line: relationships matter, so choose wisely.

One of the most perplexing things for us to wrap our minds around is how much our associations affect the way we think, act, and believe. Some become so loyal to whom they associate that they willfully sacrifice their own ambitions for the sake of friendships. This is one of the primary reasons it is so important to ally yourself with people who will empower you in the pursuit of your goals, aspirations, and ideal lifestyle.

If your friends are holding you back, then it's time to get new friends. Your associations are a critical aspect of your achievement and lifestyle objectives. If your desire is to be successful, you must associate with successful people. There is simply no way around this principle.

Take a moment to think about the five people you most associate with. Are these people the kind that inspire you, challenge you to be better, and add real value to your life? If so, great. Hang onto them. If not, it's time for a change.

"You are the average of the five people you spend the most time with."
~ *Jim Rohn*

While it is ideal to surround yourself with like-minded, positive people who want you to succeed, it is also helpful to have your fair share of critics. In fact, in my research of top achievers, I have found that while most appreciate positive feedback, high achievers value the perspective and balance of *critical* feedback because of the candid insight it can provide. In other words, most high achievers pretty much know what they're already doing right. It's what they *don't* know that helps them make the critical adjustments needed to accelerate their progress. These high-achievers, while they respond effectively to their critics, are careful not to closely associate themselves with them.

If you have ever spent any amount of time around someone who is upbeat, energetic, knowledgeable, or insightful you understand what an impact that kind of energy can have on you. Don't ever underestimate the importance of the influence of the company you keep, as it can affect virtually every aspect of your life.

Case in point...

I have been an avid fitness enthusiast all my life. Staying in the best possible physical shape has provided many benefits for me, but it doesn't always come easy. I can honestly admit that I could never have fully appreciated nor realized the benefits had it not been for the influence of other fitness-minded people who came into my life at the right time. There are lessons inside of every experience. Maintaining a disciplined physical fitness regimen for most of my adult life has taught me many things, chief among them the value of consistency and the Law of Reciprocity, which as we learned from Chapter One, tells us that the more we give the more we receive, most often in overwhelming proportion compared to our initial outlay or contribution. The people who led me to the practice field, to the running track, and to the gym have led me to countless others who have influenced some of the most powerful philosophies by which I live—philosophies that have had an effect on virtually every area of my life, even, and most especially, beyond the physical.

Your choice of friends may not seem to make much of a difference to you right now, but you can bet your bottom dollar it is the *one clear difference-maker* that will keep you stuck where you are or *catapult* you to new heights. So, stop pretending it doesn't matter and stop spending time with people who don't foster the kind of mindset that supports and nurtures who you aspire to become, and go out and create new, empowering friendships. It's easier than you may think.

If you are really serious about being the best by reaching your highest goals and objectives, you cannot afford to spend your time with people who are going nowhere in their lives, no matter how nice they are or how long you've known them. To have, be, do, or become something different you must *do* something different. In this sense, you must be perfectly selfish with regard to your future ambitions. You must set high standards with respect to your friends and associations and refuse to compromise.

Many people get into bad relationships and form useless friendships throughout their lives. This is normal and natural. There is nothing wrong with making mistakes, especially if you are young and inexperienced. But it is unforgivable to continue to stay in a situation that is holding you back from realizing your full potential. And your choice of the caliber of people you associate with will have more of an impact on *what* (and who) you become than any other single factor.

Changing your friendships and associations may seem over-whelming at first, but with a simple mindset and behavioral shift, you can easily make this happen. Besides, you don't have to totally eliminate your current friends from your life. Chances are, they will drift further away as you continue to grow and make progress toward achieving your dreams, goals, and aspirations. The primary reason for this is that you will no longer be "like" them. P.S. Don't be so concerned about the welfare and feelings of your friends that you compromise your potential. Trust me, your friends will be just fine.

Tell me who your best friends are,
and I will tell you who <u>you</u> are.

The longer you associate with someone, the more susceptible you are to their energy. We can all discern this energy. Think about a time when you met someone you were really drawn to. Now think about someone else you met that affected you in a completely op-posite way. Chances are, you did everything you could to shorten the visit or find the nearest exit with this encounter. We are more sensitive to this energy than we give ourselves credit for. Quite often, we can discern this energy within the first few seconds and without a word ever being spoken. It is this energy that most influences us. How we choose to respond to that influence is a difference-maker in our quest for personal growth and goal attainment. Choose wisely.

Some Final Thoughts

➤ **You Are Enough.** Fill in the blank… "I am (___) enough." (Good, smart, attractive, savvy, social, etc.) Align your state (body, mind, and spirit) with the newfound confidence that you are indeed "enough."

➤ **Perfection.** To strive for perfection is unrealistic. You will never be perfect, but you will *always* be enough. Never buy into the notion that you need to be perfect (or even near perfect) to strive for excellence. You are already excellent. In other words, you already have the seeds of greatness within you. All you need to do is find the source that best waters those seeds and "tend your garden."

➤ **Don't Fear Failure.** Instead of fearing failure and setbacks, regroup as quickly as possible and look for the lessons. There is always a lesson. Very often, the most successful people are the ones who learn from failure and disruption. They evaluate and get back on course quickly. It is the primary difference between success and failure. Adopt that mindset and you, too, will see *big wins* in your goal achievements.

➤ **Let's be Friends.** Do yourself a favor and reevaluate your friendships and associations…today…or as soon as possible. Then, as a matter of ensuring you stay on course and keep your dreams, goals, and aspirations centered, evaluate those friendships often and make adjustments as required.

Thought-provoking questions…

1. What do you want to do for the rest of your life? When the answer comes, do that. It is so much better to make decisions for yourself than to have other people do it for you. Do what

you want to do. It is the one place you will discover happiness—through the internal validation of your self-worth.

2. Where do you place your focus as you evaluate your self-worth? Are you consciously evaluating your self-worth, or has it become such an intimate part of you that you don't really think about it at all?

3. How does your internal self-assessment affect your external behavior? Find ways to remind yourself that others can see the reflection of your internal state through your external behaviors. Then, work on finding ways to change the internal state of your self-worth with some of the methods we have discussed in this chapter.

4. Do you find that you are protecting your vulnerability, or are you allowing it to shine as a part of who you are? Your vulnerabilities provide clues on how you can become better. Instead of protecting your vulnerabilities, find ways to use them as the strength they are to better define the purpose of your life.

Chapter Eleven

Subtle Significance

> **The major value in life is not what you get but what you become.**

Imagine having the ability to completely transform your life from where you are today to where you want to be tomorrow, and to know with certainty that the efforts you make *will* bring about the changes you desire. Since you're already using that powerful imagination of yours, take it a step further and allow your mind to create a vision so extraordinary that the very thought begins to affect all of your senses. What do you see? What do you smell? What do you hear, taste, and feel? Who are you with? How has it changed you? What second- and third-order effects has it had on your life and the lives of others? Use these powerful influencers to enhance what you see and to fuel your determined resolve to achieve your goals.

> **"Imagination is more important than knowledge."**
> ~ Albert Einstein

If you allowed your imagination to lead you, as I suspect you did, then you have just demonstrated to yourself that you have the capacity and ability to achieve *everything* you just experienced. You commanded your mind to paint a picture for you, and it responded without protest. And in so doing, you just laid down a new vision that will forever be a part of your subconscious programming. What you do from this point is completely up to you. In fact, at this point, the *only* thing keeping you from the changes you desire is the very thing you used to create your extraordinary vision—your imagination.

All too often, we place limits on the power of our imagination… by choice. We fail to realize just how much authority we have to choose, so we make *default* choices based on fear. A short-sighted vision convinces us that we have something to lose, so we hold back and make "safe" choices that prevent us from realizing the full experiences of life. We choose immediate gratification over sacrifice, apathy over effort, and caution over courage. And a great majority of people are okay with that process because it feels safe. Newsflash: safety is overrated and will prevent you from realizing your hopes, dreams, goals, and aspirations.

If you can hold it in your mind and in your heart, you can hold it in your hands.

Our achievements, and the degree to which we are successful in reaching them, are tied to the greatest power we have—our power of choice. We have a choice: Make short-term sacrifices for the sake of long-term gain, or take it easy, go with the flow, and do what most everyone else is doing to have what most everyone else has, which pretty much equates to *mediocrity*. That's not where you are, or you wouldn't be reading this book.

In over thirty years of studying the masters of success, I have found a few critical traits common among them all. These traits are not magical nor are they mythical. They are, however, significant in the difference they make in attracting the results most successful people get to experience in life while most others (the Watchers) are left to wonder why *they* are so "unlucky." The significance is subtle, hence the reason I have coined the phrase *subtle significance*. Because subtlety is all it takes to begin seeing significant change in your life. Subtlety, by the way, does not always mean things will be easy. But the results will *always* be worth it.

Successful people are proactive and decisive. That is, they consciously and proactively choose good habits and rituals over a reactive life. They are driven by the passions they have for what they do. They are detail-oriented but not so much that they allow the details to distract them or slow them down. And they don't try to do *everything* but instead do *something*—every day—that puts them at least one step closer to their desired goals and objectives.

You can do anything when you quit trying to do everything.

If we don't learn good habits, life progressively becomes more difficult. However, not even all *good* habits are created equal. Some are more powerful than others and can be a difference-maker in terms of *catapulting* you toward your dreams, goals, aspirations, and objectives. Here are four subtle but powerful habits that are sure to help you to begin to see real results in your life.

Make a Decision

The one thing that will keep you from achieving a goal of any kind is indecision. The fact that you have made a conscious choice to read this book is highly relevant and speaks volumes to your resolve in making a decision to learn everything you can to create and develop the habits required of an achiever.

Should you have difficulty making a decision, take only the minimum amount of time necessary to evaluate the best choice and *make a decision*. The sooner you make a decision, the sooner you will know whether you are on the right path. To refrain from making a decision is a decision *not* to act. Without action, your goals will never materialize.

Once you make a decision, your primary responsibility at that point is to follow-through with action and consistency. Make adjustments if you must. Your desire to go beyond ordinary and venture into the extraordinary will require your deepest resolve and commitment. But you *must* make a decision to actually do something about it by taking action. Once you have taken action, you must back it up with unrelenting consistency. Without unrelenting consistency...You. Will. Fail.

Fall in Love with the Process

The absolute best method to attaining goals is to follow a system. A system is a proven process that leads to results. Be aware, however, that you can follow the best, most proven processes and still fail. Why is that? Because the process will *always* require something from you in terms of time, money, and effort. And if you resent any part of the requirements, you will automatically be misaligned with the process.

Think about it. If you knew nothing about playing the piano but had a burning desire to play proficiently, you'd have to give something in return for the ability of playing the piano. You would likely have to commit to several hours of consistent practice over an extended period of time. If you resent that requirement in any way, you will likely not stay committed to practicing the piano.

Let's face it, success comes at a price. You must find a process you can fall in love with if you expect to be able to sustain the momentum required to achieve your goal. There may be times you disagree with the methods, prerequisites, conditions, or work required to complete the process. Unless you can fall in love with the process, you will likely take shortcuts, skip steps, or give up altogether. So, how do you overcome this to find and develop the love that's required to create the momentum and leverage the system? Read on.

"D" is for Drive

To create a sense of certainty that you will indeed reach your objectives, you've got to develop your passion to a point that you feel incomplete without having done something to connect yourself with it on a daily basis. You've got to want it so bad that you can taste it, smell it, hear it, and see it. In other words, you must be so emotionally connected to it that you anticipate the work it will take to achieve it. Of course, if that already defines you, you are well on your way to realizing your objectives. And you have separated yourself from the ordinary dreamers who are still stuck in the game of hopes and wishes.

When your momentum takes a hit—and it *will* take a hit from time to time—dig your heels in and push through it. Recognize obstacles, frustrations, and circumstances for what they are and *do not ever quit*. Find ways around obstacles and circumstance. Find people who can help you through the tough times. Educate yourself to better handle these and similar situations when they arise again. And keep moving. When you do, you will experience growth. You will experience change. And you will begin to see life differently. People ask me all the time how I wrote two best-selling novels. I tell them I just *did it*…and kept on doing it, and never ever quit, even as the obstacles revealed themselves. Within that attitude I developed an emotional connection to writing that fueled my drive to completion. In other words, I fell in love with what I was doing—the *process* that fueled my passion. When you connect with the *process* that creates your goals there is *nothing* you cannot achieve.

Ask the Right Questions

The manner in which we ask questions can make all the difference in the answers we receive and the power we give to ourselves to find solutions. Perception is everything when it comes to seeking the answers that will provide life-changing, empowering results.

Most people self-sabotage personal growth by asking the wrong questions or asking the *right* questions in a self-deprecating manner. Better stated, disempowering questions lead to disempowering answers and is *never* the right way to frame a question. Disempowering questions immediately change our subconscious thought patterns and attitudes, distorting our perception and preventing us from discovering constructive solutions. Consider the narrative that plays out in the disempowered mind...

- **Question:** Why can't I lose weight?
  Answer: Because you eat too much.

- **Question:** Why can't I do things right?
  Answer: Because you make poor choices.

- **Question:** Why am I so broke?
  Answer: Because you spend more money than you make.

On the contrary, *perceptive* questions lead to insightful, empowering, and productive answers.

- **Question:** What are the top two things I can do, *right now*, to lose weight?

- **Question:** What is a better way to accomplish this task?

- **Question:** What are three things I can do to increase my cash flow?

As we have seen throughout this book, asking the *right* questions the *right way* is empowering. The manner in which you frame your questions has everything to do with how the answer is delivered. The answers *always* come and are framed with the same packaging you use to request them. So, if you're looking for empowering, insightful, constructive answers, consider framing them *precisely* how you expect them to be delivered.

Do Something, but Not Everything

To be busy used to mean you were being productive. But that's an outdated mindset. Sure, the argument can be made that busy people get more done than most people, but we must first clearly define the distinction between *busy* and *productive.*

For a variety of reasons, busy people tend to take on more than they can handle. While this is seen by most as an honorable trait, it can, and often does, result in frustration. These very same *busy* people are also the first to tell you how much time they *don't* have, using it as an excuse *not* to get ahead in life. While it's good to be resilient, it is never a good idea to be so busy you start neglecting the things you need to get done to continue to lead a fulfilled life… and to reach your goals and objectives.

Productive people take a slightly different approach with the use of their time. They prioritize the things that *must* get done over other things that would be *nice* to get accomplished, all the while being mindful of the things that distract from what truly matters. Ironically, the majority of these people seem to be the ones taking vacations and spending time with the people that matter most in their life. So how do they find the time while most others cannot?

One word: Priorities.

The happiest people are busy, but very much in control. They are relentless (driven) in the pursuit of their goals and have a keen sense of avoiding the distractors that are designed to keep them from achieving those goals. They do *something*—but not every-thing—*every single day* to bring themselves one step closer to their desired goal or objective. They realize that *one small step* in the right direction is better than a lot of distracted steps in the wrong direction. This approach takes a bit of understanding, patience, and tenacity. At first it might not seem like they are getting much accomplished, but don't be fooled. Small changes can lead to pow-erful shifts of momentum. Consider the power of priorities and the opposing negative effects of taking on too much at once, and the choice becomes clear.

> **"I may not be where I want to be, but thank God I am not where I used to be."**
> ~ *Dr. Joyce Meyer*

So, where do you stand? As you look back upon your life, do you find that you're pretty much where you've always been? Are you ready to get some things done that bring you closer to the life you desire? Are you ready to break away from where you are to where you want to be? If so, then don't just read this book and others like it without taking the time to let the concepts and philosophies sink in.

Then take action to actually *do* something. If a real change is truly your desire, you'll take the time to use this book as both a reminder and a manual for the fundamental changes you need to enact to begin seeing results. The differences are subtle, but the results are significant.

Become an Authority

In our economic system, your income is determined by three factors: what you do, how well you do it, and the difficulty of replacing you. If you are a problem solver, your value increases. If you do it well, your value increases. When you pull it all together, you are considered to be an authority. But what makes someone an authority? Is it education, experience, effort, perseverance, exposure, excellence? Yes.

One of the qualities of successful people is that, at a certain point in their lives, they decided to make a commitment to excellence. They make a decision to be the absolute best at what they do. They decide to step up, make short-term sacrifices for the sake of their long-term goals, and invest the amount of time, money, and effort necessary to become very good at something. As a result of this decision, they pull away from the pack of average performers and move themselves from ordinary to extraordinary. The result of their newfound position of excellence comes with a reward. The reward is manifested in the way they feel (intrinsic), the number of lives they affect (intangible), and the manner in which they get paid (extrinsic), based on their extraordinary value. Some of these extraordinary performers have landed into income brackets where they earn three, four, five, and ten times as much as their peers who have decided not to make this commitment. And so can you.

*"You can learn anything you need to learn to
achieve any goal you desire to attain."*
~ *Unknown*

There are no pre-defined limits on what you can accomplish, except for the limits you place upon yourself. If you decide to become an authority, an expert, or to join the top achievers, there is nothing on earth that can stop you from getting there. Will it be easy? It could be, but it will most likely require a lot of work and commitment. Fortunately, most everything worthwhile takes time and a lot of work to accomplish. Yes, you read that correctly, I said *fortunately*. You see, if it were easy, most everyone would be inclined to do the task. So, it is *fortunate* for you that excellence comes with a price of admission. If you have the resolve to do what most others are simply unwilling to do, to have what most others are unable to have, then you will be the *fortunate* one. If you want it badly enough and are willing to work long enough and hard enough, you can, and most certainly will, achieve anything you can think of.

*"To achieve something that you have never
achieved before, you must become someone that
you have never been before."*
~ *Les Brown*

Once you make a conscious decision to become the best, the question you must first ask is *how*? The fact that countless people have gone from ordinary to extraordinary is proof that you can do it as well. Many of these people weren't blessed with the natural talent or abilities *you* currently have. In most areas of life, the only requirement to travel the path leading to excellence and success is hard work and dedication. Even those with a natural ability or specific talent must work hard to cultivate that talent and garner the attention of others to stand out.

Start Here

Here is the critical question for the rest of your life as it applies to achieving a goal or objective of any kind: *What one skill, if you developed it and did it better than everyone else, would have the greatest positive impact on your life and the lives of others?*

This question is the fundamental focal point for every aspect of your personal and professional development. Your answer to this question, as it applies to each and every area of your life, is essential to you achieving excellence.

Keep asking yourself the following: "What one skill, once developed and accomplished in an excellent fashion, would have the greatest positive impact on my income and on my future?" If you are at all unsure about the answer to this question, seek the advice of others you trust. It is absolutely essential that you discover the answer to this question and then put all of your focus and energies on improving your performance in every deficient area supporting your answer. As a reminder, this can take a lot of effort, time, and work. But those elements are the very same elements that separate you from the ordinary.

Once you discover those areas you need to develop or improve upon, you will have the clarity you need to get started. Then, *get started!* Create a goal, set a deadline, make a plan, take action on your plan, and then do something *every single day* to improve your skills. As you do, you will become an authority. Do this for each and every aspect of your personal development plan, and you will become an authority in each respective area, and you will be rewarded accordingly.

185

Acquire the Skills

In today's global society, your required knowledge and skill changes by the second as it becomes obsolete at a faster rate today than ever before. Your earning capacity can be an appreciating or a depreciating asset, depending upon whether you are growing or simply "cruising along" during the constant state of change.

The good news is that when you start to systematically upgrade your knowledge and skills on the road to success and achievement, it will be as if you are in a race and you are the only one who is running. You'll quickly move ahead of the crowd and into a position among the leaders where things become clear and life takes on a deeper meaning. Meanwhile, most everyone else is simply strolling along, doing just what they need to do to keep from losing what they have become accustomed to. As you gain more insight to this, you will realize that *they* are actually working harder to maintain their status quo while your time systematically begins to free itself from the bounds and encumbrances of an ordinary life.

Begin your action to excellence by asking the question, "What additional knowledge, skills, and information do I need to become an authority and reach my goals?" Project yourself forward three to five years and imagine that you are one of the very best, highest paid people providing the value or service you seek to provide. What would have to have happened? What would you have to have done, learned, or accomplished to reach this point? What skills would you have had to master? Consider the following short story as you ponder these questions...

Sir Edmund Hillary was the first man to climb Mount Everest. On May 29, 1953, he scaled the highest mountain then known to man—29,000 feet straight up. He was knighted for his efforts.

He even made American Express Card commercials because of his extraordinary accomplishment. However, until we read his book, *High Adventure*, we don't understand that Hillary had to *grow* into this success.

You see, in 1952, he attempted to climb Mount Everest but failed. A few weeks later, a group in England asked him to address its members.

Hillary walked on stage to a thunderous applause as the audience acknowledged and recognized his attempt at greatness. But Edmund Hillary saw himself as a failure. He moved away from the microphone and walked to the edge of the platform where he made a fist and pointed at a picture of the mountain and exclaimed in a loud and determined voice,

"Mount Everest, you beat me the first time, but I'll beat you the next time because you've grown all you are going to grow…but *I* am still growing!"

Identify Your Gifts and Talents

There are many ways for you to identify and determine your unique gifts, talents, skills, and natural abilities. Keep in mind that you will always be the best and happiest at something you enjoy doing. If you could, you would do it without compensation. This goes right to the point made earlier on falling in love with the process. Doing something that comes easy to you brings out your very best and ignites a tremendous amount of satisfaction, fulfillment, and enjoyment when you are engaged in that particular activity. Consider the following among the many ways to identify your gifts and abilities:

➤ The activity brings you joy and satisfaction. It is not work, even when you must spend hours taking your skill to the next level. You spend hours in your lane of passion without eating or sleeping, losing track of time, hour after hour, because you get so involved. You have developed a passion for the activity that continues to enhance your knowledge and skillset from unique to extraordinary.

➢ You have a natural inclination to master the skill. You may actually forget when and how you learned it.

➢ You align yourself with others in the same field or interest. You want to be like them, be around them, and emulate them in every conceivable way.

If these descriptions apply to anything you are doing, or anything that you have done in the past, they are directly connected to what you were uniquely put on this earth to do.

Do not ignore the call you hear, or
you will miss your calling.

Your natural talents are easy to develop. They are programmed into your subconscious mind. They are what you were put on this earth to do. Your objective is to identify and develop your natural talents and abilities to enhance the quality of your life and the lives of others. In so doing, you will have discovered the very reason you are here—to fulfill a purpose, your unique purpose. What an extraordinary opportunity to experience something few people ever consider, much less experience in their lifetime.

Most skills are complementary. That is, they are interdependent upon each other. For example, to fully execute a particular skillset you must be able to effectively employ one skill at a certain level in order to use other more predominant skills at yet another level. I cannot tell you how many times I have had to learn and develop skills that I did not particularly enjoy in order to fully execute my predominant skillset. But this is part of the price we must all pay to be able to achieve excellence in our primary skill.

One Skill Away

You could be just one skill away from doubling your productivity, performance, and income. You may only need to increase or enhance your skill level in one area to experience a breakthrough to a higher level. Skill enhancement leads to increased ability and capability, which allows you to move about more freely within your predominant skillset.

It is quite common that, if you are weak in a particular skill, you will tend to avoid taking action to develop that skill. Resist negotiating or rationalizing yourself away from the inherent responsibility you have to enhance your abilities.

If the ability you seek to develop is important enough, you can learn it. You don't always have to master an ability to enhance your predominant skillset. Oftentimes, a fundamental understanding is all that is required for you to enhance your skillset and get beyond a delay or obstacle. The very *worst* decision would be to allow yourself to be held hostage for any period of time because you lack a single skill that is ultimately overcome through determination and perseverance. Don't let this happen to you. If you absolutely cannot overcome the obstacle, reach out to an expert or authority who can help you through it. There is *always* a way around setbacks, obstacle, and delays.

> *"Anything worth doing well,*
> *is worth doing poorly at first."*
> ~ *Zig Ziglar*

Whenever we start something new, we tend to do it poorly at first. In fact, we *expect* to do it poorly. We feel clumsy and awkward. We feel inadequate and inferior. These experiences are a normal part of the evolution of growth that eventually lead to greatness. There is always a price associated with success. Whether you actually *pay* that price or *enjoy* that price is irrespective of the work required to ultimately reach the pinnacle of your goals. I'd be remiss if I did not ensure clarity in the message that it often takes hard work to master the difficult skills you'll need to move to the top. Do *not* fear the work, because it is the *work* that will be the difference-maker between you and your closest competition.

The RLA$_2$ Formula

Among the many recommendations and methodologies available to you, the **RLA$_2$** formula for mastering any skill is among the easiest to remember and implement. It is fairly simple, straightforward, and it works *every single time*.

Read. First, create a source library and read and watch everything you can expose yourself to that promotes the skill you aspire to build. Read or watch something from your source library every day, even if only for 15 to 30 minutes. Knowledge is cumulative. The more you expose your mind to the richness of knowledge, wisdom, and inspiration, the more you learn. The more you learn, the more confident you will become as your skills increase.

Listen. Second, listen to educational audio programs (podcasts, instructional programs, personal development masters, inspirational speakers, etc.) while traveling in your car or on an airplane. The average driver spends 500 to 1,000 hours each year in the car driving to various destinations. Turn your traveling time into learning time. You can become one of the best educated people in your field by simply listening to audio programs in your car. Add airline travel time to that if it applies, and your learning curve accelerates. You cannot beat the return on investment of this part of the formula.

Attend. Third, attend seminars, webinars, workshops, and presentations. Considered to be among the most expensive in terms of a financial commitment, this form of learning provides an opportunity to benefit from the highest rate of return on investment. These methods very often put you at arm's length from those who have mastered a skill you seek to enhance. Personally speaking, I have never failed to gain value from this style of personal development.

Act. And the final step of the formula is to *practice what you learn* at the earliest possible opportunity. Every time you hear a good idea, take action on it. The person who hears one idea and takes action on it does more for their success than a person who hears a hundred ideas but takes action on *none* of them.

Practice Makes Perfect

It is not practice that makes perfect; it is *imperfect* practice that eventually makes perfect. The premise behind this statement is the more you practice what you are learning—even if imperfect at first—the faster you will become competent and skilled in a given area or discipline. Your willingness to do something, every single day, that supports your goal or objective is critical to the outcome you expect to achieve. Never allow perfection to become an excuse for taking action on anything. More often than not, we must act with the information we have at hand and adjust as necessary. This action philosophy supports the consistency factor mentioned throughout this book. Also, the more you practice, the more your confidence increases. The more confidence you have, the faster you will overcome any feelings of inadequacy, and the faster you will master a particular skill. To be clear, even the masters are not always perfect.

Make a decision today, right now, to join the top performers in your desired field, specialty, or endeavor. Determine who they are, what they know, and more importantly, *how* they do things differently that sets them above the rest. Determine the specialized knowledge and skills they have developed and begin by doing what they do. Remember, anything that anyone has already proven can be done, you can do as well. No one is better than you, and no one is smarter than you. The very fact that the top people in your field were at one time not even in your field at all, is proof that whatever they have achieved, you can achieve yourself, if you simply set a goal and work at it long enough and hard enough. There simply are no limits.

Establish the Right Relationships

As noted in previous chapters, the right relationships are critical to your success. No one person operates in a vacuum. Once you have clarity on the type of people, groups, and organizations whose help and cooperation you will need to achieve your goals, it is time to get busy establishing those relationships. If you don't consider yourself a social person by nature, take action to learn more about how to engage with others without coming across as someone with an ulterior motive. Social interaction is imperative to your success. A great start is to strive to always treat people with kindness, courtesy, and compassion.

Never make the topic or agenda about you or your business unless it is expected (you are attending a networking or chamber of commerce meeting). If you follow this one rule of thumb, you will *always* establish meaningful relationships. Seek first to offer something of value for a person's time and attention. And never pre-judge a person on first-impressions, although you should always assume that *you* will be judged that way. Think about how many times you may have secretly pre-judged a person only to find out *after* you have drawn your conclusions that the person was of a totally different caliber, profession, or income level from which you had wrongfully assumed. The best you can do is to learn from this by becoming more aware of people and by reserving judgment until you are more certain. So, resolve to make a great first impression. Smile, look people in the eye, and project confidence. And by all means, try to remember a person's name. This establishes *rapport* and sets the groundwork for meaningful relationships.

Some Final Thoughts

> **Make a Decision.** It has been said that every journey begins with the first step. That first step is absolutely critical in bringing about the realization of a goal. The greatest power you have is the power of choice. You will *always* have the power of choice. No one can take that from you. Choose wisely, take action, and follow through with unrelenting consistency.

> **Ask the Right Questions.** Your ability to properly frame a question shapes the manner in which you approach your plan of achievement. Be mindful to ask *empowering* questions that will help you to see all solutions in a positive manner. Doing so opens the window of creativity, which helps you establish momentum and consistency. (You may begin to notice a theme here: consistency wins.)

> **Stay Consistent.** If you haven't read it enough already, it's worth mentioning one more time (it's that important). Your ability to do something every single day is absolutely essential to the accomplishment of any goal or objective. Consistent action—in any form—assures progress, knowledge, insight, and the progressive skills you need to accomplish your goal.

> **You Don't Have to Be an Expert but You Must Become an Authority.** Recall the 3 factors to becoming an authority:

what you do, how well you do it, and the difficulty of replacing you. Once you establish a certain level of insight, knowledge, and skill on any given topic, your journey to goal accomplishment becomes easier. Your increased level of awareness, insight, knowledge, and skill become familiar. As these things become increasingly second-nature to you, they provide room for you to continue to grow. Another benefit that comes about is that people take notice and begin looking to you for answers. This progressive personal growth establishes you as an authority and makes it easier for you to reach your goals.

➤ **Remember the RLA$_2$ Formula.** Practice the RLA$_2$ Formula (on a consistent basis) and you will continue to improve as a person and will be better equipped to achieve any goal you set. This simple formula will help you create solid habits and rituals that are essential to an effective plan of goal achievement.

Thought-provoking questions…

1. Imagine… Imagine the accomplishment of your goal. What do you see? What do you smell, hear, and taste? How do you feel? How has your life changed? Who else is affected by the accomplishment of your goal? As you think about your goal, be sure to connect it to a compelling vision you have of how you see yourself *after* you have accomplished it. Your imagination is so powerful it can literally shape the outcome, the timing, and the conditions of every goal you set.

2. What are the obstacles and limitations that are preventing you from making a decision? A decision speaks to your resolve on making progress toward the accomplishment of your goals. Action produces results, but there can be no action without a decision to act.

3. What are the elements of the RLA_2 formula? Committing the elements of the RLA_2 formula to memory will help remind you to put at least one of these elements into practice every single day.

Chapter Twelve

Fast Forward

"The longer you wait, the longer it takes."
~ Robin Sharma

Speed matters. In fact, it has been said that success *loves* speed. Think about it. When was the last time you heard someone say they got great results from getting there *last* or getting there *slow*? If you want to leverage the results you're getting, you need to get there first...or at least early enough to have a shot at getting the best results. The best way to do just that is with speed on your side. This is true in virtually every area of life...

> ➤ If you want to get the best deal on an investment property that just hit the market, you need to get there first. The only way to get there first is to get there fast.

> ➤ If you want a shot at getting a date with the man or woman of your dreams, you need to get there first, else you will find yourself in a line of others competing for their time and attention.

> ➤ If you want a chance to get that promotion you've had your eye on, you need to get there first.

> ➤ If you want to win the race, you need to get to the finish line...first!

As we learned in the previous chapter, time is a precious commodity. The best use of your time is absolutely essential to goal achievement. Compressing your timeline enables you to get to your goals faster. Speed brings along with it the lessons required to stay ahead of the competition in terms of tactics, techniques, and procedures—fundamentals I learned long ago while serving in the US military. Along the way, you will continue to discover various means to improve the nature and experience of your journey. And with speed, you will discover them faster than your competition, giving you first-mover advantage. On the contrary, when you procrastinate, you tend to lose your enthusiasm...and your advantage.

There are no speed limits on the road to excellence. The ones who are decisive, driven, consistent, and quick typically win. So, once you make your mind up on the direction you must go, then do precisely that—go!

Some people "throttle back" because of a fundamental apprehension they have of not knowing the next step. The sad part about this is that they typically start slowing down before they ever complete the step they are on. Don't let that be you. Trust that the next steps will be revealed to you precisely when you need them, if not sooner.

The more results you have in a given time period, the more motivated you become to harness that power and keep going. Of course, the opposite is just as true. Slow and infrequent results bring on frustration and doubt, which brings about a tendency to set things aside for another time, which we can all agree generally leads to giving up altogether.

Compression

There are many things you can do to accelerate your personal and financial goals. One of the most powerful practices that has worked especially well is one that has taken more people from mediocrity to magnificence than any other single method. It is simple, fast, effective, and virtually guaranteed to work—as long as you take action and commit to consistency. Want to know what it is? Excellent. Keep reading...

We have all heard the phrase, "You become what you think." This powerful mantra serves a universal truth that provides a philosophical and psychological edge to success far beyond the obvious. I have always believed that whatever you can hold in your mind, you can hold in your hand. This, too, is a universal truth that is intimately connected to one of the most important actions you can take to compress your goal achievement timeline and produce results faster than you ever have.

Many people today talk about the importance of positive thinking. And while that's all good, and positive thinking is important, it is not enough. Left unchecked, positive thinking can quickly degenerate into positive *wishing* and positive *hoping*. Instead of serving as an energy force designed for inspiration and higher achievement, positive thinking can become little more than a cheerful attitude. We need to be careful to support our positive thinking with the action steps necessary to support the positive *movement* of progress toward our goals.

To be focused and effective in goal attainment, positive thinking must be transformative. That is, it must evolve past positive *thinking* and into positive *knowing*. You must absolutely know and believe, in the depths of your soul, that you are going to be successful at achieving your specific goals. You must confidently step forward with the resolve and assurance that you *will* achieve the goals you have set. You must be so resolute and determined, so convinced of your ultimate success, that nothing can stop you. Okay, great! So, how do we do that?

Everything you do to program your subconscious mind has an effect on whether or not you make progress toward your goals. The method I am going to share with you actually *leverages* your results and greatly increases the speed at which you move from where you are to where you want to be. Does that thought capture your attention? Excellent!

The great Napoleon Hill famously said, "Whatever the mind of man can conceive and believe, it can achieve." We use the powerfully philosophical nature of this quote to set up the magic that will assure the inevitable successful achievement of any goal you can imagine.

Thought Seed

I have been using the principles of effective goal-setting most of my life. For years, I worked away at my goals, writing them down when I thought of a new goal and then periodically reviewing, updating, and reaffirming them. This was enough to make an incredible difference in my life.

It wasn't until years later that I learned of a subtle shift in technique, which would change my life. I discovered that, if writing down my goals once or twice was powerful enough to provide the results I was getting, it should be even *more* powerful for me to write down my goals more often. While some experts recommend we write down and review our goals once a year or once a month, I discovered the amazing power of writing my goals *every single day*. This, I quickly discovered, accelerated the results I was seeing and significantly compressed my timeline to achievement.

So, here is the technique. We're going "old school" with this method. Hey, there's a lot to be said about the old school methods and how powerful they can be (and still are to this day).

Okay, so, find a small notebook you can keep with you at all times. Each and every day, open your notebook and write down a list of your top goals. You can write down one goal, or you can certainly write down more than one goal, but you must *at least* write down your number one goal—even if it is the same goal as yesterday and the day before. Try to do this without referring to your previous day's writing if you can. Do this every day, day after day. As you do, several remarkable things will happen. For starters, you will become more intimately involved with your goal, which feeds one of the most powerful aspects of who you are—your subconscious.

Writing your goals is akin to planting a seed—I call it *thought* seed—into your subconscious. Many people have no idea just how fertile the subconscious mind is. Plant just about any thought there and it manifests. Keep planting the same thought seed and transformative behaviors begin to form. The very thought of your goal is the seed that leads to the maturity of your thoughts and beliefs about what your life would look like once you have achieved your goal. The action you take to write it down is the catalyst that helps water the seed. By taking action every single day, you are cultivating a virtual Garden of Eden that will lead to the realization of your goal.

As you begin to experience more frequent results, the content and quality of those results will have a transformative effect on how you begin to think, believe, and act. Your life will literally change as you become empowered to do even more to bring about the achievement of every one of your goals.

The Process

Make today your Day One. Starting today, write down your goals. Write your goals as if you have already achieved them. This is important. If you use words such as "I will" or "I wish" or "I want," your subconscious automatically categorizes your goal as something you "will" or "may" achieve. This, I have found, places your goal into a future state and perpetually just beyond reach. In other words, it "will" never happen. Be sure to keep the narrative of your goals positive. Finally, make sure your goals are personal.

Here are a couple of good examples of a well-written goal...

Example 1:

It is July 4, (year). I am sitting on the porch of my 3,000 square-foot dream home with my family at my side. I am grateful for all we have accomplished this year together. Our six-figure passive income has allowed us to help so many people and has provided a financial freedom for us to travel to places we could have only dreamed of just one year ago. I smile as I watch the most magnificent sunsets from where we sit in our back yard. I have a greater peace of mind than I have ever had. I have mastered the art of (insert your passions here). As a result, I am happy, healthy, wealthy, and wise. I am thought of as an authority in the field of (insert your passions here). I am able to help so many people and be here with my family to enjoy the full experience of life. And that is my ultimate reward.

Example 2:

It is September 15, (year) as I read the details of my undergraduate diploma from the University of (school or institution). I am debt free because of the actions I took to work part-time while I attended classes. I have several solid offers for jobs and am grateful to have come so far. I have direction and purpose in my life, and I am grateful.

Example 3:

Stop right here to create YOUR first *personal, positive,* and *present* goal. Use this simple, but powerful, exercise as your Day One. Then, do it again tomorrow…and again the next day…and the next.

Allow your imagination to paint a clear picture as you read the narrative of your goals. This is an important part of the process as your imagination has the highest influence on your subconscious. Once you have written your goals and have read them, put the notebook in your pocket or a special place where you can return to it at will, at least daily. A highly recommended ritual I prescribe is to review your goals at least twice: once in the morning and once before you go to sleep at night. This method programs your mind for the day ahead and provides a nice visual as one of the last things you think of at night.

Go through the same process the next day. Refer to your previous day's list if you must. Write your goals and read them. Allow them to take root. Repeat the next day…and the next…and the next.

Soon you will discover that you won't need to refer to your previous day's list because of the increasing acceptance by your subconscious. This is a huge leap forward in the transformative process of your mind because your subconscious begins to believe what you're telling it as a truth or reality. Once the subconscious believes something as a truth, some amazing things begin to happen. Your thoughts, beliefs, and actions begin to change to best align with the goals you have systematically programmed into your mind through the daily ritual of writing and reading them. You will begin to feel more confident, driven, and assured that you will indeed achieve the goals you have set because things will begin to manifest around you unlike before. The best part is, you will begin to notice the changes as they occur. And, as you do, you will be compelled to continue doing the things that have brought you here.

This daily ritual *will* change your life. And it won't take long at all. You see, your subconscious mind is like a sponge. Once it absorbs the story you consistently tell it, it begins to change you. Your mind will become increasingly aware of opportunities, ideas, and insights. You will begin to attract the people and resources in your life that will help make it easier to achieve your goals. Your rate of progress and success will increase and become exponential. As this will be a new experience for you, be careful not to resist the changes because this will become your new normal.

Make it Personal, Positive, and Present

As I briefly mentioned earlier, the manner in which you frame the context of your goal matters. Writing your goal as if it were already accomplished puts your subconscious on notice that it must conform to the new standard. The subconscious takes your convincing narrative and automatically compares it to the current state of what is. When this happens, your subconscious suddenly realizes that your life is incongruent with where you are versus where you desire to be. At first, your subconscious attempts to reject the new narrative...until you keep telling (and showing) the new story. This temporary phenomenon explains the anxiety some of us feel when we consider doing something new with our life. This is also where the magic of your daily thought seed ritual comes into play. Tell your story enough times and you (your subconscious) begin to believe it is true.

> *"When we deny the story, it defines us. When we own the story, we can write a brave new ending."*
> ~ *Brené Brown*

Be mindful to construct the narrative of your goal so that it is *positive, present, and personal.* As mentioned earlier, I think we can all acknowledge the power of positivity. Generally speaking, most of us would much rather hang out with someone who is positive than someone who is negative. A positive story is inspirational, invigorating, and inviting. Listening or reading something positive disarms us and puts us in a position of acceptance. It also changes our state of mind, which ultimately changes our state of being.

A narrative that is written in the present tense stimulates the imagination and compels us to adopt a state of mind that begins to manifest the very thing we desire to achieve or become. Be sure to use power words to start your goal statement, such as, "I am...", "I earn...", "I have...", "I live...", "I help..." I don't know about you, but just writing these words puts me in a brand new empowered state of mind!

Finally, come to terms with the fact that *this is personal*. There's no way you are any good to anyone else if you are not fulfilled. Some people may mistake the personal nature of your drive as a self-centered attempt to have, be, do, or become something they are not. Newsflash: it doesn't matter what they think. Only *you* know the true nature of your drive and motivation. The person you ultimately become as a result of your goal achievement is what truly matters. Refer to the power words once again and notice how each begins with the word "I." This powerful one-letter word commands the full attention of your subconscious and ignites a flame so bright it simply cannot be ignored. Use this one word often, and your entire life will change.

The Force is With You

When you take action to physically write your goal—no matter how big or impossible it may initially seem—you activate an incomprehensible series of universal forces that make the impossible and the improbable possible.

This is not the time to make conservative goal declarations. Put aside fear, doubt, and uncertainty. These emotions have no relevance in the outcome of your goal...unless you allow them to prevent you from accepting the successful outcome of your desired aspirations. Push past your typical self-imposed boundaries and apprehensions as you describe your goal. Go beyond what you would normally define as *reasonable* in terms of what you *expect* will happen to what you actually *desire* to happen. The point here is to compel your subconscious to grow while conditioning your mind to accept the new reality you deserve.

Just Do It!

All that is required to make this method work is for you to *just do it*. So, get a small notebook of some kind and faithfully follow through each and every day. Remember to write your goals in the positive, present, and personal tense. In a matter of time, you will begin to see how your whole life will have transformed and how you are comfortably stepping into the new reality of your life.

If you are skeptical about this method, then you are not alone. You've got nothing to lose and everything to gain. I have never met anyone who has applied this method to their goal achievement plan who has reported anything short of significant and measurable success.

Force Multiplier

You can leverage the effectiveness of this method with a couple of additional techniques. First, after you have written down your goal in the positive, personal, present tense, write down at least three actions that you could take immediately to achieve that goal.

For example, if your goal is financial, you could write the following: "I am a $90,000 per year earner." Or, "I am an expert at teaching others to how to (_____)." Immediately underneath, write the following: 1) I make time every day to learn more about money and the way it works; 2) I plan every day in advance; 3) I always focus on my most important tasks first; 4) I eliminate distractions to help myself concentrate, single-mindedly, on the tasks that directly support my goals and objectives.

Whatever your goal, you can easily think of three supporting action steps you can take immediately to help achieve that goal. After all, as we already know, action is the catalyst for movement and progress to occur. Writing the action steps helps you to program them into your subconscious. Before long, you will find yourself taking the steps you wrote down, oftentimes without even consciously thinking about them. With each step you take, you will move ever closer toward your ultimate objective. This, ladies and gentlemen, is called growth. And it is a precursor to achievement.

Some Final Thoughts

➤ **Success loves speed.** Let's face it, unless you're the kind of person who likes to go fast, speed can be intimidating, especially when the path ahead is not as clear as we would like it to be. The way goals work, however, goes completely against the grain in terms of what we consider "normal" when it comes to what we expect will happen versus what actually happens. So, set your plan in motion and don't let up on the accelerator. The path ahead will come into view in plenty of time for you to navigate effectively.

➤ **Food for thought.** Consider using the "old school" thought seed formula to accelerate your results. Grab that pocket notebook and create a new ritual of writing your goals every single day. Make time for this, and the entire landscape of your results will change.

➤ **3P X 2/D = SUCCESS!** Remember to make your goals personal, positive, and present (3P). Review your goals twice a day (2D), and step into the successful fold of achievement!

> **Leverage your results.** Once you establish a ritual of writing and reviewing your goals every single day, don't forget that there's more you can do in terms of adding fuel to the fire of your acceleration plan. Look for small actions you can take to create incremental victories for each one of your goals. Break down large tasks into smaller ones. For example, if a given task typically takes a month to accomplish, think of the things you can do on a weekly or daily basis that will assure your completion within a month. Do this for each of your goals, and they will not seem so overwhelming and intimidating.

Thought-provoking questions...

1. Have you ever considered how speed factors in to your goal-getting actions? Have you been guilty of throttling back as you consider the next steps to take? Have you been guilty of delay tactics, setting things aside you know you could be doing but just haven't been for one reason or another? Stop wondering why other people are getting results and start getting them yourself. Do more and do it now. Why are you waiting?

2. When do you want success? When would you like to reach your goal? If you're like most people, your answer is "right now" of course. Well, if "right now" is your expectation, then "right now" is when you should get started.

3. When you visualize your goal, are you thinking in terms of "I will" or "I am?" The difference is subtle but significant. Command your subconscious, starting "right now," to think in terms of "I am," and your results will indeed begin to change. Paint a clear picture using the positive, personal, and present nature, and your subconscious will begin to manifest the conditions for you to commandingly step into the reality of what you aspire to achieve.

Chapter Thirteen

Don't Settle

"You get no more and no less than what you believe you deserve. Don't settle."
~ Dan Millman

There comes a time in everyone's life when they evaluate their own successes. Part of that evaluation takes into account the sacrifices made contrasted against the outcomes they have achieved. This self-evaluation leads to a value judgment we place upon ourselves and a determination of where we go from that point forward. If we conclude that the sacrifices we have made for the successes we have enjoyed is too much, we tend to either pull back or reevaluate our *why*—that reason which has driven us to this moment of our lives. If, on the other hand, we determine we could be doing *more* to achieve the goals we have set for ourselves, we look for ways to improve upon the efforts and tactics we have employed to achieve the lifestyle we currently have and push ourselves even more to a life we desire and truly deserve. Whichever camp you find yourself in requires an honest acknowledgement on whether you are truly happy and fulfilled. In either case, if you settle for anything less than what you honestly desire and deserve, you will most certainly find unhappiness and discontent. Therefore...

Don't Settle

As mentioned in an earlier chapter, when you set a goal, life will invariably ask something of you in return. It may be money, resources, time, or any combination (or even all) of these. Things will sometimes become difficult or present themselves as a challenge, oftentimes requiring something of you that you may or may not have, know, or completely understand. You will face frustration, anger, fear, and maybe even a bit of anxiety as you struggle to find solutions. These things (and more) will bring you to a crossroads—a decision point where most people stop and give up or settle for a "normal" life as they look back on how "easy" things used to be. It is here—where the average person turns away and gives up—that you must take one more step, put in one more hour, invest one more dollar, or make one more phone call to achieve a goal you *know* will materialize, set you apart from everyone else, and significantly change your life forever. Whatever it is, however impossible it may seem, never give up, never give in, and never ever settle for less than you know you deserve.

Knowing the limits of our own capabilities is essential in the careful and calculated consideration of our ability to achieve the things we desire. If, for example, we desire to achieve something we are not physically or intellectually prepared for, we must either do the work it takes to become prepared or choose another goal. It is beautifully simple yet frustratingly unambiguous.

Achievement brings with it both tangible and intangible results, as is pointed out in Chapter Two, *Return on Investment*. One of the highest forms of return manifests itself through a transformative process that changes the very essence of who we are as we evolve and grow toward achievement. This process offers a spiritual reference to a level of human cognition or awareness that evolves through exposure to the experiences (and lessons) of life. An important part of the spiritual reference is a reawakening of our sense of knowing that everything is connected. And, if everything is connected, then it only goes to prove that your actions are directly connected to the results you achieve.

Better Than Average

One of the most common questions I receive, in one form or another, while talking with people on the topic of personal achievement is, "What can I do to become better than average?" To which I answer, "Plenty." For starters, I get them to think about whether they are using their time constructively. Most people waste a lot of time because they're simply busy with the wrong (think unproductive) things. There are others, however, who stay busy with a laser-focused mindset on being productive. It makes me think of a common phrase I have often found to be very true.

"If you want something done,
give it to a busy person."
~ *Benjamin Franklin*

This phrase, originally quoted by Benjamin Franklin, has stood the test of time and is more appropriate today than ever in history because of the sheer number of things competing for our time and attention. It is largely believed that the reason busy people are more reliable is because they have systems (rituals, habits, principles) in place that keep them from veering off course. They think intuitively, methodically, strategically, and purposefully. They build in margins for unforeseen inevitabilities. These people don't settle for less, and if they accept an additional task, they already know they are well able to meet or exceed the expectation because of the success and reliability of their system.

Here's the unvarnished truth of the matter when it comes to personal reliability: *You are as reliable as your word.* If that stings a bit, then perhaps it stings for a reason. If it doesn't sting but resonates, then you are likely a reliable person.

So, find opportunity gaps in your schedule and fill them with actionable tasks you can conduct to put yourself in the path of your goals. If your goals require credentials, arrange your schedule to earn the credentials. If your goals require you to connect with people of influence, take the time to learn how to interact with people of influence. Then build in the time it takes to connect with those people.

Another amazingly simple approach to becoming better than average is to be willing to do more than anyone else. This philosophy builds upon the principle of effective task management within the confines of your available time. In fact, as I write these words it is late evening on a weekend. My wife is in bed fast asleep and has been for a few hours. Yet, here I sit, doing a little more than everyone else in terms of what it takes to write a manuscript that will lead to the published book you are now reading.

When someone says it cannot be done, or something is not possible, use that as an opportunity to be the first to prove them wrong. Not for the sake of proving them wrong but for the sake of proving to yourself that it can be done *despite* what others may think, *despite* the odds, the difficulty, or the time it may take for you to accomplish. This is the fundamental nature of the requirement for goal-getting.

Learn more than anyone else by exposing yourself to the kinds of material that will empower you to become that which you intend to become. Look, studying can be enjoyable if you read the right material from the right sources and the right authors, or if you watch the right videos that affect the fundamental nature of who you are into whom you intend to become.

A vital part of becoming better than average is to never surrender on the goals you desire. Sadly, most people give up as soon as things get tough, only to later complain that they never achieved the goals they set out to obtain. A test of your willingness to achieve your goals *will* present itself sooner or later. If you desire to achieve those goals, you will have to pass the tests. It will be hard. You will feel like crying, be frustrated, angry, and exhausted. You will also feel like quitting or find yourself looking for easier alternatives. I cannot tell you the number of times I have faced these types of challenges in my adult lifetime as I set out on my goal-getting ventures. Each goal presented new and unique challenges, which I had to face, figure out, and overcome in order to achieve. I recall the voice of my organic chemistry teacher who perhaps put it best when he characterized these daunting challenges as "rites of passage." Indeed, many of these challenges are *rites of passage* in that they weed out the weak-minded tire kickers and unqualified curious onlookers who would otherwise crowd the field for which you have qualified. Your right of passage also rewards you with the knowledge, skills, and confidence only the well-deserved rightfully own as part of stepping up to the challenge of doing whatever it takes to be where you desire to be.

When you settle for less than you truly deserve, you become an accomplice in your own dissatisfaction. The sad irony is that while most people believe things will be easier when they settle for less than they know they are capable of achieving, things actually become more complicated. On the contrary, as you begin making decisions that reflect what you desire from life, you will begin to feel better about yourself. The better you feel, the easier it becomes to focus on the things that help bring your goals to fruition: gratitude, self-improvement, awareness, joy, learning, and love.

Here are five ways to stop settling and begin to align yourself with the elements of change that lead to the attainment of your goals.

1. **Stop rationalizing the behavior of others.** Let's face it, there are times when other people do things to you that af-

fects your ability to be at your best. Your ability to function outside of this influence matters. Instead of rationalizing why people are the way they are, try speaking directly to what hurts you. If those people refuse to hear you, or if they dismiss or invalidate you, and you accept it, you are settling for less than what you deserve.

2. **Not getting what you want is not a personal curse.** Your personal narrative has a huge influence on the outcome of your dreams, goals, and aspirations. If you tell yourself that you are somehow cursed (unlucky, unfortunate, unqualified, etc.) by forces beyond your control when challenges or obstacles appear, you make yourself vulnerable to settling for less. Those points of view concede themselves to defeat from the outset and do nothing to promote the attainment of your goals. The reality is, while we may have a pretty good idea of the goal we desire, we have no way of knowing just how the achievement of that goal will materialize.

3. **Being alone does not equate to abandonment.** The true strength of your character is knowing yourself. The best way to get to know yourself is by embracing opportunities of solitude. I'm reminded of a quote that summarizes this philosophy...

"When everything has left you, you are alone.
When you have left everything, there is solitude."
~ Schiller

Until you are able to be alone to discover the best of yourself, you will be of little good to anyone else. You will settle for the wrong friends and continue to wonder why you find yourself in a perpetual cycle of unhappiness and stagnation. Break the cycle by refusing to settle for less than you truly deserve. Spend the time getting to know the one person who can change it all—yourself.

4. **Express your desires—and do it often.** No one gets what they want without fully *knowing* what they want and expressing it to others in a manner that affects the outcome. Your ability to influence the hearts and minds of others rests in the absolute personal conviction of your desires. If you are not fully convinced you cannot expect anyone else to be. Express your desires to everyone. Declare them aloud. Put the universe on notice so the forces of support and resolution can find a clear path to you.

5. **Don't accept what you don't want.** Have you ever heard the term "yes man?" A huge part of settling is to agree to everything, most especially when you'd prefer saying no. If you agree to things you don't really want, you are building a life that is incongruent with your personal identity.

Everything Ends

You have one life. There is a beginning and an end. What a tragedy it would be to look back upon your life knowing you settled for less than you truly could have...*should* have achieved if only you had chosen to live differently. You have the power to make that choice right now. When I'm faced with a decision to pursue or relent...to settle...I am empowered with the knowledge that there is nothing in this life that should be powerful enough to cause me to settle for anything less than I deserve. Nor should you.

Ten years from now, it won't matter what brand of shoes you wore, what kind of car you drove, or what neighborhood you lived in. All that truly matters is how you lived, how you loved, who you touched, and what you learned along the way. Deep down, you already know this. Yet, today, a great many of you are easily distracted and derailed by the insignificant aspects of life.

You give too much of your time to meaningless distractors. You step through your day cautiously, with skepticism and cynicism, a great majority of the time looking for ways to escape it all. You take your relationships for granted. You give in to fear and doubt. Why?

Because you're human.

But, every bit of that can change if you will just embrace one facet of life—awareness. As we age, we tend to become more aware of the fragility of life. This insight has a tendency to foster an appreciation for the things we often miss in life because of the many distractions that abound. But you don't have to wait for this insightful wisdom. You can have it right now.

Don't look back upon your life with regret. Consciously decide, right here and now, that you will *not* settle for anything less than you truly deserve. There will never be enough time to do the things we want to do, say the things we need to say, or live to the extent we believe we should live. Yet, your awareness of the present moment will reveal things to you that will enhance the quality of every aspect of life, far beyond your ability to comprehend...until you step into awareness.

Some Final Thoughts

> ➤ **Don't settle for less than you know you deserve.** You know yourself better than anyone. Therefore, you alone know if and when you have settled for less than you deserve.

> ➤ **Be ready, willing, and able to give whatever it takes to accomplish your goal.** Achievement will always require

something of you. Knowing that at the outset puts you in a position of power and advantage as you set out with the right mindset to experience the journey to success and achievement.

> **If you know you can achieve second-best then you can certainly achieve better.** Achievement in any form is a win, but achieving that which you know is the absolute best of your hopes, dreams, and aspirations is something worth striving for. Don't settle. Never accept what you don't want in exchange for what you truly deserve.

> **Eliminate distractions.** Do something every day to advance your goals. When you do, turn off your phone, turn off your e-mail and social media notifications, and get to work. Soon, people will wonder how you are getting so much accomplished when it is all really a rather simple formula of eliminating distractions.

Thought-provoking questions...

1. Are you willing to give whatever it takes when life calls upon you to give something in return for the goals you have set?

2. Are you doing everything it takes to be better than average? Are you willing to do more than anyone else (average-minded people) to include working longer, staying up later, learning more, and investing more to reach your goal?

3. Are you aligned with the elements of change as they relate to your goals? From mindset to physiology and intent to resolve, you must be willing to step squarely into the lane that best supports the elements of change in order to achieve your objectives.

4. Do you fully understand the concept that everything ends? If you do, you will be empowered by the knowledge that everything you hope to accomplish in this life rests upon the fragile and predictable nature of the timeline you have here on this Earth. Be determined not only to achieve the very best life experience but to leave an empowering and inspirational legacy for others to emulate long after you are gone.

Chapter Fourteen

It's Go Time!

**"Small deeds done are better than
great deeds planned."**
~ Peter Marshall

Everything you hope to accomplish in life lies in wait for you to act. You are solely responsible for the construct and content of your life. Every choice you make—from the use of your time to the selection of your mate—makes a difference. So, if you've been blaming everything and everyone for your "circumstances," that stops right here, right now.

If you are not happy with your life, the only one who can change things is you. Change is one of the most difficult things for people to accept because change introduces a new unknown into our life. Most people are uncomfortable with the unknown because they are afraid of what it will ask of them.

Unfortunately, most people view change as a threat or as something that will require sacrifice or payment. The fact is, they're right. Change *will* require something from you, but it will always give you something in return. This simple but powerful truth is based on the *Law of Reciprocity*, which tells us that if we give something of ourselves, we will receive (often in overwhelming abundance) something in return.

In order to achieve most anything in life, the one critical ingredient is action followed by more action and backed by even more. Without action, nothing happens. Without *consistent* action, nothing lasts. You can have the best plans, the best intentions, the best team, and the best conditions, but if you don't act, you will never make any headway toward the goals and objectives you set. In other words, you must *do* something.

How many times have you heard someone say that they would like to do something "someday?" You may have even said it yourself a time or two. Well, the last time I checked, "someday" is not on the calendar. Instead of declaring that you will get around to doing something "someday," why not set an actual date or timeframe? Why not *today*?

The Focus Factor

Okay, so action is necessary, but once you begin taking action, you need to keep taking action. I have mentioned throughout this book that a lack of consistency and an unwillingness to follow-through are among the biggest obstacles to achievement. Without them, you will quit, give up, and fall well short of what you truly deserve…if you finish at all.

There are doers and there are procrastinators. The doers understand that consistency produces results. They also understand that, to best fuel consistency, they need to predict the conditions in which they are most likely to quit. This is important, so please don't overlook this part of the goal-getting strategy. Predicting that part of the journey where you are most likely to quit gives you an advantage over circumstance. We all know circumstance can be extremely convincing in getting us to think twice about our motivations. Quitting too early has been the nemesis of so many would-be success stories. Don't let it apply to yours.

The 40% Rule

The U.S. Navy SEALs have a "40% rule" they live by to overcome the urge to quit. This rule is a special operator's credo to mental toughness. The rule explains that, when our mind is telling us that it's time to quit, we are really only about 40% depleted. This is by design, as our mind is designed to "protect" us from danger. What it perceives as dangerous, however, may or may not always project an accurate snapshot of reality. The fact still remains that we have an astounding 60% capacity (mental, physical, and/or emotional) left within us to continue on and push past the ruse of negative mental images caused by circumstance.

I'm not sure how you see it, but when I discovered this 40% rule, it resonated with me. I look back upon how most times (thankfully), I found something inside of me that kept me going when everything else tried to convince me to quit. Again, this is a ruse, a psychological programming malfunction designed by circumstance to steal your dreams. This ruse is the infamous "wall" you may have heard people talk about when they face seemingly insurmountable odds. Those who have *hit the wall* can attest to the amazing feeling of accomplishment they have when they find something within themselves to help them push *past* the wall to finish what they started. Athletes, researchers, first responders, military…and you. Yes, even you will inevitably encounter "the wall." And when you do, remember, you are only about 40% done. Keep going!

The procrastinators, on the other hand, believe they will eventually have time to accomplish the tasks that are required to achieve their goals and objectives. Their good intentions are easy prey to distractions and other priorities caused by circumstance that invariably appear throughout a given day. Well, good intentions have no part in a well-structured plan of action. Good intentions are nothing more than an excuse to put off for another time what should be done *right now* in order to begin seeing results. The excuse-makers have no idea what the 40% rule is because they quit before they even come *close* to the wall. They don't plan their journey and, as a result, have no idea where they are likely to face the wall and feel like quitting. As a result, they are typically overcome by circumstance and end up quitting or readjusting their goals to fit the circumstances.

To avoid giving up when you have so much left to give, start by identifying the biggest challenge or problem facing you today as you make your way to achieving your goals. Imagine that the challenge has been sent to test your resolve and desire to reach the finish line.

One of the most important aspects of preparing for inevitable challenges is the development of options. Your ability to overcome circumstantial obstacles is only as effective as your ability to develop actionable alternatives. Whatever your goal, you must have choices at the ready when challenges and obstacles appear. You must have more than *one* choice you can make in every conceivable situation. Don't ever allow yourself to be limited with only one course of action when you need it most. And decide right now that you will *never* give up, even when the challenges emerge. After all, you have a 60% reserve waiting for you to call upon to get you there.

Action = Progress…every time

The best measure of progress is *action*. Even if you take the wrong action or are somehow inaccurate in completing a task correctly, your actions shape your discipline. As your discipline matures, your consistency increases…and, so too do your habits and rituals. I can tell you from experience that every one of my significant achievements have been brought about by a determined, laser-like focus, that propelled me toward my goals and objectives, even beyond my own expectations. Another noteworthy result of your achievements will be in how others perceive your accomplishments as somehow extraordinary when, in reality, the only difference is your determined focus and follow-through. So, make a difference by being different. Finish what you start. Do not quit. And you *will* reach every goal you set.

The focus formula is quite simple: eliminate distractions, predict your point of failure, prepare for it, accomplish something having to do with your goals every single day, and find balance in your life. If all you do is concentrate on the tasks you have to accomplish, you will burn out, become resentful, and eventually give up on your goals as you end up convincing yourself that it's just not worth the effort. Action, supported by determined focus, will save you hours, weeks, and months of confusion, mistakes, and losses in terms of money, time, and energy. Just make sure to reward yourself by doing something you enjoy once you have taken action toward your goal and begin to see progress.

A Matter of Clarity

It's easy to become overwhelmed when we step back and consider the entirety of our goal. Don't try to figure out steps two, three, and four before taking and finding your way through step one. Instead, just take that first step and things will gradually become clear to you each subsequent step of the way.

How you manage your 24-hour day has a lot to do with the progress you make toward your goals. Your ability to focus on tasks closely associated or in direct support of your goal helps you to see the overall picture of your strategy with greater clarity. The increased perspective will reveal gaps or opportunities for you to use your time more efficiently. In fact, psychologists generally agree that the way we use our time is linked to our emotions in terms of the values we have developed, which directly affects feelings of happiness, confidence, power, and personal satisfaction with where we find ourselves in life.

The good news is that, no matter how disorganized you may have been in the past, or how much you tend to procrastinate, or how prone you are to distracting activities, you can change. You can become more efficient, effective, and productive by modeling effective habits and rituals that influence your core beliefs. You can go from confusion to clarity and from frustration to focus with just a couple of small changes in your habits and rituals. One of the rituals I highly recommend is to develop a daily task list.

Task List

There's something to be said about "old school" methods we first mentioned in Chapter 12. One of the old school methods I routinely use is a hand-written daily task list. Much like the daily ritual of writing down our goals, the daily task list represents a microcosm of small tasks you must do in order to accomplish larger, more significant tasks, and eventually reach your overall goal.

Tasks are the steps you must take on your journey to achievement. Now, your list doesn't have to be hand-written, so long as you create something that puts each task in front of you (visually) every day. I use my list as a basic tool for effective *task management*. I list tasks by priority and place a square block next to each item (like this: □). I use the square block as a place to "check off" the item as I complete each task. This simple method helps me to focus on each task as I tackle it and gives me a sense of satisfaction when I check it off as I complete it.

Establish Your Priorities

Given how many distractions we have coming at us at any given moment throughout our busy lives, it is a wonder we can accomplish anything at all. Only you can take responsibility for the accomplishment of the things it will take to achieve your goal. No one else will (or should) do it. Make it personal. Own it.

When creating your list of tasks, it is important you establish your priorities by placing the most compelling task as the highest priority. A top tier task demands attention. Your top task may be one that can be accomplished in a relatively short amount of time or it may require several days. Try not to reprioritize or move to the next task until the top task is complete. A completed task is a marker that serves as evidence of your progress.

Perhaps the best single word in the pursuit of your goals and the time and attention you must dedicate to it is the word "No." Saying *no* to any demand on your time that is not the most valuable use of your time at the moment is one of the smartest decisions you can make to leverage the effect of your outcome.

> *"The things that matter most must never be at the mercy of the things that matter least."*
> ~ *Goethe*

Your decision to begin a task is a declaration of your commitment and determination to achieve your goal. Never trivialize what it takes to start. Committing to act on a task is a choice you freely make to avoid distractions and other competing tasks. It is the precursor to every task that follows and ultimately adds to the shape and manner of your outcome.

Consider the clear differences that exist between success-minded people and most everyone else when it comes to tasks. Successful people attack high value tasks first. Theirs is typically a strategic perspective that produces results that drive the tactical or low value actions that support the broader perspective. Success-minded people are not easily distracted by low value tasks. They understand that while some low value tasks add value to their strategy, the low value tasks often take care of themselves or can be assigned to others willing to serve a support role.

We are all free to choose the method we adopt. But if the method you're using isn't working well for you, a new approach may be in order. After all, your choices determine the progress and overall successes you experience. Choose wisely.

It's a Matter of Time...or Is It?

The fact is, you can't manage time; you can only manage *yourself*. That's why task management has less to do with managing time and more to do with self-discipline, self-control, and self-mastery. Self-management requires you to make the best choices and decisions necessary to enhance the quality of your life and work as you follow through on your decisions to take action. How you go about accomplishing tasks is completely up to you...so long as you actually take action to complete the tasks associated with your goal or objective. Only then will you begin to see things develop. Time is relevant only to the extent that your tasks are measured against the goal you intend to achieve.

Time can be a valuable ally in terms of compelling you to act to meet a deadline or desired state. Leverage it, but don't ever become encumbered by it. As we have already seen throughout this book, effective goal-setting strategies should include near-term, mid-term, and long-term goals. With that in mind, it's best for you to take the same approach with respect to your goal-getting strategy. Your daily task list should directly support your immediate goals, which indirectly support your mid- and long-term goals. Keep this in mind as you create your daily task list. In most cases, your daily task list will naturally become a part of your daily rituals and routine once you begin seeing the results of how it brings about the realization of your overall goals and objectives.

Determine precisely where you can carve out time in your day to dedicate to your goal. Even if all you have is 30 minutes every other day, then claim that time as "goal time," then resolve to claim those precious 30 minutes as time you will consistently allocate to working on your goal. Structure your dedicated time allocation so that all distractions and interruptions are held to an absolute minimum. Enlist the help and support of your family or roommates so everyone understands the importance of this time period.

The extra one-and-a-half to two hours a week can be a difference-maker in terms of the cumulative progress you make. After all, you'll be taking action on something you would have previously believed you didn't have time for.

It is a lot easier to formulate a plan of action once you have a clearly-defined schedule in front of you. The importance of a calendar was first mentioned in Chapter One. And here it is again for emphasis. This method is critical in helping to convince your subconscious of the importance you place on your goals.

As you attempt to find the time slots available on your calendar, be quick to recognize the activities you are currently committed to that can be considered unproductive. This mindset forces us to prioritize the importance of our goal against the tasks to which we're currently committed. Consider things such as non-productive computer time (social media), watching television (social influence), and extracurricular activities that detract, rather than attract, success into your life.

To begin, take an overarching account of your current obligations and rituals. In other words, what are you currently doing, say, on a weekly basis? It may help to print your calendar with space that includes things like your work hours, your family obligations, physical fitness routine, and personal time. Most everyone—even the busiest and most obligated among us—can find some "white space" in their schedule to conduct activities that support a goal or objective. I like to think of the old adage, *if it is important enough, you'll find the time.*

> *"Every great accomplishment of mankind has been preceded by an extended period, often over many years, of concentrated effort."*
> ~ Earl Nightingale

Make it a habit to connect with your goal every single day before you approach your dedicated time slot. This refreshes the mind and invigorates the soul by reconnecting your subconscious with your goal. After all, your goal is the very reason you have restructured your life. Then, simply get to work. I suspect you will be surprised at just how fast the time goes by as you work on the tasks associated with your goal, especially as incremental results begin to emerge.

Speaking of results, be certain of the results you are looking for when conducting the tasks associated with your goal. Nothing will frustrate you faster than a lack (even a perceived lack) of results. Are you writing a book? If so, what are the incremental results you are looking for? What milestones have you set? Are your results a certain number of paragraphs per day? Are you learning a new skill? How many instructional courses will you have to complete before you can earn a certification in your new discipline? Clarity is paramount in all things, most especially in the pursuit of goals. Be absolutely clear of the results you seek, and your results will continue to propel you forward.

Once you begin seeing the results of your actions, you will also become more perceptive of *unproductive* time. A question likely to emerge is one that asks whether what you're doing at any given moment is the best use of your time. Your responsibility at this point is to get out of your own way and allow the winner in you to emerge. There comes a time when you have to choose between turning the page or closing the book. That time is now. Are you ready? If so, it's go time!

Some Final Thoughts

> **Don't fear or attempt to avoid change when change is the very thing you seek.** The accomplishment of your goals will bring change to your life. Some kind of change will occur whether you want it to or not. The question then remains, will you be navigating the winds of change or reacting to them? Most people believe it is easier to adjust to the changes that occur "naturally," when in fact it is far easier to play an active role in the changes that occur.

> **Action is the catalyst that drives change.** Most people think that without action, nothing happens. The reality is that life still happens. It just doesn't happen for you…it happens to you. The best way to assure a steady progress toward the goals and objectives you have is to take an active role in their development. Remember this when things seem to slow or stall. There is always opportunity to do something to keep the momentum going.

> **Apply the 40% Rule.** Use this rule to remind yourself that you have twice the capacity to sustain your drive and feed your tenacity when you hit the proverbial wall. You will find your second wind if you remember to look for it. It will only be available if and when you summon it.

> **Focus and follow-through.** Taking the first step toward your goal is often not as difficult as taking that step again… and again…and again. The clear difference-maker between results and frustration is consistency. Get past this hurdle, and you will have mastered the art of achievement, pure and simple.

> **Find a method that works for you to track your tasks.** Even the busiest among us should make time to keep up

with the tasks we need to undertake to achieve our goals. Prioritize your list and accomplish your high value tasks to see consistent results.

> **Make good use of your time.** Time is the great equalizer in the world of success and achievement. Those who make the best use of their time make the biggest strides and achieve the biggest gains. Give yourself permission to use everything at your disposal to manage the tasks that are necessary to accomplish your goals. Recall the "old school" list creation approach and use that...or make up something that works well for you.

Thought-provoking questions...

1. Creating a goal is one thing. Acting on it is another matter altogether. If you have taken the time to clearly define your goal and have established a plan to achieve it, you must be ready to follow through with action if you ever expect to achieve it. The question, however, is not a matter of readiness but one of willingness. Your clear plan of action substantiates your *readiness*. But your state of mind governs your willingness. How badly do you want it? Bad enough to carve out time, resist distractions, and commit everything you have to achieve it? Bad enough to change the fundamental nature of your habits and rituals until you see the momentum begin to appear? Vow, right now, to prove to yourself that you already have the will to act. You can do this!

2. Have you taken a good, in-depth look at the path you must follow to achieve your goal? Have you predicted the conditions where you are most likely to quit? Have you pre-

planned a method or mindset to use more than your 40% when you will need it most?

3. Are you doing everything you can to make steady progress toward your goals and objectives? Are you making the best use of your time? Make no mistake, you will achieve what you are willing to take the time to achieve…no more and no less.

4. Are you measuring your progress? Are you attacking the highest priorities first? Have you taken full responsibility for the progress of your goal? You must find the inner strength and be able to tap that source at any given moment, most especially when things seem stacked against you. It is here, at this precise moment, that the achievers are separated from the dreamers. Which one are you? Declare your victory *before* you see the results, for it is here where the true winners emerge.

Putting It All Together

*"Great things are done by a series of
small things brought together."*
~ *Vincent Van Gogh*

Throughout this book, you have been given a glimpse into the
powerful process of setting and getting goals. You either learned
or were reminded just how powerful it is to declare your goals, how
to create or recreate them, write them down, and act upon them. At
the outset, I made a bold declaration, telling you that the successful
achievement of your goals is not only possible but *certain*. My hope
is that you now understand how I could have made that declaration
with confidence.

In this book, you have learned perhaps the most comprehensive
strategy for setting and getting goals that has ever been comprised in
one book. You have also been reminded of the differences that exist
between those who achieve and those who don't. As you know by
now, the differences are subtle, but significant enough to draw stark
contrasts between the two. By practicing the rules, principles, concepts, and philosophies contained in this book, you can accomplish
more in the coming months and years than most people accomplish
in a lifetime. By adopting a fresh new mindset, you can step forward

with confidence, knowing your goals are all but certain, save for the permission you give yourself to succeed.

Now it's time to put it all together. It's time to step into that fresh new perspective we learned about in Chapter One. The perspective that not only reminds us of the fundamental nature of goals but of just how powerful our goals are to the condition and construct of our lives. It is also time to take a step back to look at the philosophies, principles, and practices of this book from a broader perspective. It is from that perspective that we are better able to see the entirety of it all and to begin building a personalized plan of action without becoming overwhelmed by the process.

The premise of this book is to remind you of the inherent power you have to be in full control of your life while you enjoy the pursuit of your goals. It all begins with a state of mind that serves to set the conditions from which to think, plan, and build the life you want to live through effective goal-setting and goal-getting. It is with these two overarching aspects that we create a life we desire through the achievement of our goals.

Remember to begin with the most compelling reason you desire your goal—your why. This, by far, is of utmost importance in the fundamental construction of your goal. Everything is built upon the basis of why you desire something. Don't set out on your journey until you know for certain *why* you desire something. Once you know why, no one or nothing can stop you.

Today, there are so many new and exciting developments taking place around us at an ever-increasing pace. The options and choices we have at our fingertips leave us with no good reason or excuse to fall short of our goals. Find good resources and leverage them to your advantage. These are essential steps that help get you going and *keep* you going during occasional deflation periods and setbacks.

Goal Mind

There are no problems you cannot solve, no obstacles you cannot overcome, and no goal that you cannot achieve by tapping into your creative mind—your Goal Mind. To help keep you going, I recommend you plug into sources that remind you of the inherent power you have with respect to achieving all of your dreams, hopes, desires, and aspirations. Books like this one will help you immensely. Social media is another great source, if used wisely. My only caution is that you don't allow it to distract and consume the time you should be dedicating to the advancement of your goals. Balance and moderation are best practices. So, use social media and never allow it to use you.

If you're on Instagram, seek out people who add value to the mindset you strive to feed. If you would like to keep up with me, I can be found on Instagram **@goal.mind** and **@garywestfal**. I make it a point to frequently post something positive, inspiring, or insightful you can use to keep your subconscious mind on the right track and in line with the principles, concepts, and philosophies supported by this book.

G-Life Magazine

I write a monthly blog dedicated to the concept and philosophy of introspection, the process that calls for us to look within ourselves for the true source of strength we all inherently possess. You can find *G-Life Magazine* on my website, or on Medium.com at: **https://medium.com/g-life-magazine**. Be sure to opt-in to receive a notice when I publish a blog or provide valuable updates. There are many ways to become a part of the Goal Mind experience, not the least of which is by simply sending me an e-mail: info@garywestfal.com . I do my level best to answer all of the mail I receive. Simply tell me to add your name to the list, and you'll begin receiving relevant content to support your Goal Mindedness!

Your Greatest Power

I have spoken to many people across the world in many different cultures. And I have found several similarities despite the cultural differences. Of the most powerful commonalities we all have is one that is largely responsible for our ability to survive—our desire to discover the best of ourselves and to leave this world better than it was when we arrived.

If I could pass along only one thought that would help you to gain more insight, become more inspired, find more success, and discover the key to happiness, I would tell you that life is a series of choices. With each and every choice we make, we write the narrative of our lives. The most powerful tool you have is your personal power of choice. No one can ever take that from you. So, make a conscious choice today to write down your goals, visualize them as if they have already happened, and do something *every single day* that brings you closer to realizing them.

This advice, if you make a commitment to follow it consistently and without fail, will be of more help to you in achieving your goals than virtually anything you could ever imagine. This philosophy has changed my life and the lives of countless others. It will change yours as well.

The very best to you, always.

Gary Westfal

It's Time for Action!

"Action is the catalyst that creates accomplishments. It is the path that takes us from uncrafted hopes to realized dreams."
~ *Thomas Henry Huxley*

If I've said it once I have said it a thousand times, for change to occur *you* must change. The only way you can change is to take some kind of action. If you've taken the time to read this book, you have already accomplished the toughest part—getting started. So, consider it your official start to the momentum you will build along the path of your journey. Your willingness to spend time reading the concepts, truths, and philosophies in this book have armed you with more knowledge than your closest competition and has set you on a corrected course to the intentional desires of your heart.

If you're like most people, you read the book, got motivated, inspired, and encouraged by the possibilities that await. Don't stop there. Re-read any chapter in this book and you'll likely re-experience some of the same images, visions, inspirations, and creative thoughts you had during your first time through the passages. The reason for that is simple. Your hopes, dreams, goals, and aspirations are a vital part of the internal programming that defines who you are and who you are yet to become. This is personal. The things you're seeing and feeling are emerging for a reason. They are glimpses into the inspirational aspects of what awaits you…*if and when* you act upon them. These glimpses provide increasing clarity the more you immerse yourself into the process. Once you gain clarity, you gain focus. With focus you gain *power and dominion* over the changes you need to make to achieve your dreams, goals, and aspirations. Change begins with action. And action, consistently practiced, produces life-changing results!

The absolute best to you as you embark on your journey with a whole new mindset…your *Goal Mind!*

Your reviews and recommendations are vital to the success of every author. If you enjoyed reading this book, please help spread the word by leaving a positive review on Amazon and other social media sites and by recommending this book to others.

How to Apply the Goal Mind Principles to Business

An Unadvertised Bonus Chapter

Many of the Goal Mind principles are as applicable to business as they are to individuals. In fact, when applied in a business environment, the Goal Mind principles can be *leveraged* to produce extraordinary results. The reason for that stems from the alliances that are formed and the collaborative effect that naturally emerges among like-minded members of the team. I've written more on this in a **bonus chapter** you can find at the link below. I think you'll find it to be an incredibly useful addition to the main ideas covered in this book.

You can download this chapter here:

http://www.garywestfal.com/bonus-chapter/

About the Author

G ary Westfal leapt onto the writing stage when his first criti-
cally acclaimed novel, *Dream Operative*, achieved an Amazon.
com No. 1 ranking in its first year of publication—a phenomenal
feat for a first-time novelist. A frequent and lucid dreamer, Gary
began documenting his dreams in order to better understand the
alter-conscious phenomenon and himself on a deeper level. His
writing has been consistently compared to seasoned thriller writers
like Brad Thor, Tom Clancy, Vince Flynn, and Joseph Finder and
to best-selling personal development leaders such as Mike Rowe,
Chris Widener, Andy Andrews, Jack Canfield, and Mark Sanborn.

He is a former United State Air Force air traffic controller with an eye for detail and a passion for serving others.

Gary publishes his work under his own label, the G-Life Enterprises Corporation, and he creates the concepts for his cover and jacket designs in collaboration with some of the best traditional and graphic artists in the country. His website (GaryWestfal.com) provides visitors with examples of his knowledge and creativity as a writer/novelist. As a speaker, his personality and charisma are contagious attributes, whether in casual one-on-one conversations or speaking to large audiences. His lecture and presentation skills are best described as confident, engaging, and articulate.

He is the creator and chief contributor to *G-Life Magazine* (medium.com/g-life-magazine), a periodic blog providing thought-provoking topics seeking to enrich the lives of his readers by challenging them to think deeper, look within themselves for answers, and be mindful of the value of the present moment. The blog offers a fresh perspective on personal empowerment and covers a wide range of human-interest topics while providing a canvas of thoughts and introspection leading to a better understanding of the elements connected to true happiness, balance, and harmony in life. He frequently speaks to audiences about human performance and practical business applications using inspirational narratives.

When Gary isn't writing, he can be found watching an alluring sunset while sharing a glass of wine with his wife on the beaches of the Emerald Coast of Florida.

To be a part of Gary's inspirational blog and to receive other timely information from him, be sure to visit his website, where you can become part of the conversation with one simple click.

Garywestfal.com